Empirical Assessment in IHL Education and Training

Empirical Assessment in IHL Education and Training

Better Protection for Civilians and Detainees in Armed Conflict

Jody M. Prescott

ANTHEM PRESS

Anthem Press
An imprint of Wimbledon Publishing Company
www.anthempress.com

This edition first published in UK and USA 2021
by ANTHEM PRESS
75–76 Blackfriars Road, London SE1 8HA, UK
or PO Box 9779, London SW19 7ZG, UK
and
244 Madison Ave #116, New York, NY 10016, USA

British Library Cataloguing-in-Publication Data
A catalogue record for this book is available from the British Library.

Library of Congress Control Number: 2021940240

ISBN-13: 978-1-78527-948-5 (Hbk)
ISBN-10: 1-78527-948-3 (Hbk)

Cover image: Cynthia Petrigh / Beyond Peace

This title is also available as an e-book.

For my wife and daughters.

CONTENTS

ACKNOWLEDGMENTS

I have been very fortunate over the years to have worked with outstanding friends and colleagues, and I am indebted to many of them for their assistance in putting this book together. I am grateful to Susan Mitchell for her invaluable help, when we served together at the US Army Command & General Staff College, in creating and analyzing the international humanitarian law (IHL) training survey we used with the Class of 2002. I also wish to thank Cynthia Petrigh for being so generous with her time and her willingness to share her experiences and materials from instructing soldiers in IHL, and Keisuke Minai for sharing his insights on the use of war video games in IHL instruction and responding to my follow-up questions with such thoughtful detail. Finally, I am particularly grateful for the insightful comments and corrections of my readers Adam Gittleman, Victor Hansen, Mette Hartov, Antonia Hultin, Brian Ketz, Lone Kjelgaard, and especially Dieter Fleck, who gave me my first real opportunity to write and experience a rigorous editing process so many years ago. Any assessments and mistakes, of course, are my own, and this book represents the views of no US or other government agency, or of any defense organization.

INTRODUCTION

I was a legal advisor in Kabul for a year, starting in the summer of 2008, working for the US general who commanded the regular international and US forces in Afghanistan. The deployment came late in my time with the US Army, and it was there that I learned the reality of applying IHL in a complex conflict that often defied easy legal and political description. We were a small office of American, British, and Canadian military attorneys, and there were never quite enough of us to meet all the demands for our work, whether it was in claims, contracts, the rule of law, or, most importantly, IHL.

That meant that even though I was the office chief, I would sometimes find myself in the dynamic targeting cell[1] as an action officer, providing real-time legal advice as targets (groups of men or individuals) were engaged by air assets. I knew the engagement protocols because I had helped train headquarters units rotating into Afghanistan on them when I served as an observer/trainer at the Joint Warfare Centre in Norway. Using them for real was different, though, and sobering. Likewise sobering was the job I usually saved for the evenings after my regular work was done, reviewing investigation reports of civilian injuries and deaths in engagements and at vehicle checkpoints.

The commander wanted to know whether there were any trends or patterns that could be identified from these reports that could be addressed in training or rules of engagement (ROE) guidance to soldiers to reduce the tragic instances of civilians being harmed. Reflecting my professional bias, I recognize now that I read those reports through a legal lens, tinted both by my perspective on the ROE and what I saw as the soldiers' understanding of them in their uses of force. I rarely found something in an individual case that I believed I needed to report to the general from this viewpoint—but neither did I create a spreadsheet to track the specific details of the cases to see whether I could discern anything from looking at the legal and nonlegal data as a whole.

My deputy took a broader view in these cases as to what had happened and why. Often, when I shared with him what I had found, he would note what he saw as leadership issues in how the ROE were being applied. He would question what he saw as a lack of tactical patience in the decision-making by soldiers, which he related back to training in their ROE, which, of course, had to be consistent with IHL. In this sense, he also had concerns about the values that undergirded their training. I understood his points, but to me what still mattered, above all else, were the legal standards the soldiers were expected to meet, because that is where I believed the focus of IHL and IHL-related education and training should be.

It has taken a while, but I no longer believe that. Instead, I now think that lawyers need to step back and integrate their work with that of other professionals who have roles to play in delivering this education and training, such as mental and behavioral health specialists, statisticians, ethicists, and counselors. These multidisciplinary teams need to focus their combined efforts on educating, training, and supporting military leaders, particularly young leaders at the small unit level, both officers and noncommissioned officers (NCOs). This focus must be broader and more intensive, more systematic, and it cannot consist simply of more training on the law. Further, to ensure that IHL training is as effective as it can possibly be, its content and delivery must be driven by data throughout the unit training and deployment cycle.

Most importantly, this training must be led by leaders. Its purpose must be reinforcement of the shared positive professional and emotional bonds between leaders and soldiers, and its goal must be soldiers' internalization of IHL principles as part of a sound, collective military identity consistent with our democratic values. Accomplishing this goal likely depends upon leaders modeling ethical decision-making processes that take into account the need to resolve conflicts between what might seem like competing positive values of equal weight at first glance, and how to weight those values to come up with proper solutions. As the final step in this approach, leaders must provide meaningful feedback on the analysis of this training to the led.

Some might be concerned that such an approach is too intangible and that it would be too difficult to objectively measure accomplishment of these training objectives. On the contrary, I believe the reinforcement and internalization of a shared professional identity can and must be measured, and when the results show that the education and training is not working as expected, it must be changed in ways that the data indicate are promising options. Although I recognize that this approach would require new resource investments across militaries to work well, I also believe that these commitments, if they are carefully planned in advance, can be flexible and affordable.

This book's scope is modest. It takes a case study approach in looking at different programs and courses over the past 20 years involving the empirical assessment of attitudes, perspectives, and behaviors related to IHL education and training effectiveness and compliance. From a larger IHL point of view, it does not directly address the application of the law between combatants. Instead, it focuses on the treatment of those not involved in combat, such as civilians not directly participating in hostilities and detainees irrespective of their IHL status. From the standpoint of basic IHL principles, I am most concerned with humane treatment and distinction between combatants and those not in combat. Perhaps surprisingly, as I will begin to explain in Chapter 1, I also see an important role for the older (some might say obsolete[2]) IHL concept of chivalry, reinterpreted in a modern context as honorable professionalism.

To best understand how an approach driven by data, led by leaders, and oriented toward values could foster a culture of willing and professional compliance with IHL among soldiers, we will need to dive deep into the data of these different case studies. I ask for your patience with me in this because it is only by getting into the data itself that the analysis of it will make the most sense outside the specific contexts of the case studies themselves. I recognize in making this request that I have left an important question open: Why is such an intensive approach necessary? Militaries around the world already provide IHL instruction and training to their forces, consistent with their nations' obligations under international law,[3] and have done so for decades. To answer that, it is helpful to begin by briefly reviewing the historical development of IHL and contemporary initiatives that have the shared goal of increased protection for those not in combat.

Treaties of Protection and Their Impacts

World War II was marked by mass atrocities against civilians and prisoners of war, on a scale humankind had not previously experienced. The Holocaust in Europe, the deaths of an estimated 3 million Soviet prisoners of war at the hands of the Nazis,[4] and the deaths of perhaps as many as 20 million Chinese attributable to the imperial Japanese forces[5] stand out as grim milestones of savagery against those who were either civilians or who were no longer in the fight. The 1949 Geneva Conventions were one of the most important responses by the international community to these tragedies,[6] and they forged new and clearer protections for civilians caught up in the occupation of their countries by hostile forces, and for former combatants who had effectively left the battlefield sick or wounded, or as prisoners of war.

These protections are particularly strong regarding international armed conflict. The nations that universally agreed to these measures in the wars that they might fight against each other, however, were much less keen to apply them to conflicts that might occur within their own territories.[7] In an important advance for the protection of all victims of armed conflict, though,

Common Article 3 of all the conventions established a minimum baseline of humanitarian protection for all victims of armed conflict, irrespective of whether the conflict was international in nature or a non-international armed conflict.

After 1949, the world moved from dealing with the aftermath of World War II to the conflicts that occurred during the Cold War, which included armed struggles against Western colonial powers and apartheid regimes, and proxy conflicts between the West and the Soviet Union and its allies such as the wars in Vietnam. These conflicts resulted in a massive toll of casualties who were not combatants,[8] and they were responsible in large part for the international community reconvening in 1977 to promulgate the protocols additional to the 1949 Geneva Conventions.[9] The Additional Protocols generally expanded the protections available to combatants and those who were not fighting in both international and non-international armed conflicts.

Many countries ratified these treaties, especially Additional Protocol I. A number of countries, including the United States, did not. The United States has, indirectly perhaps, acknowledged that many of the Additional Protocols' provisions have become applicable as a matter of customary international law.[10] This reflects a consensus in the international community that important rules governing the conduct of hostilities during international armed conflict are now largely applicable in wars not of an international nature.

Like the Common Article 3 approach, each of the 1949 Geneva Conventions contains an article that places an affirmative duty on signatories to inform their populations about the treaties.[11] For example, Geneva Convention III, dealing with prisoners of war, requires "the study thereof in their programmes of military and, if possible, civil instruction, so that the principles thereof may become known to all their armed forces and to the entire population." Further, military or civil authorities who are responsible for prisoners of war are required to "possess the text of the Convention and be specially instructed as to its provisions."[12]

Additional Protocol I reiterates these requirements.[13] It also clarifies the concept of special instruction by requiring signatories to provide legal advisors to "military commanders at the appropriate level" on the application of these treaties "and on the appropriate instruction to be given to the armed forces" on the treaties.[14] In addition, it also places an affirmative duty on commanders to ensure their subordinates are "aware of their obligations" under these treaties.[15]

Importantly, steps to increase protections for those who are not in combat have not been restricted to the states that signed these treaties. International organizations, such as the United Nations, nongovernmental organizations of an international character, such as the International Committee of the

Red Cross (ICRC), as well as smaller nongovernmental organizations have played a crucial and complementary role over time in developing more narrowly focused treaties that have as a common goal the greater protection of victims of armed conflict. A good example of this is the Ottawa Convention prohibiting the use of land mines, which resulted, in large part, from the efforts of an individual, Jody Williams, and the International Campaign to Ban Landmines.[16] Simply put, achieving greater protection for civilians and detainees is everyone's business, and the nations of the world are not the only actors with a stake in making this happen.

Less Fruitful Efforts

Not all efforts in this regard have been so successful, however, and a brief review of two of the more significant initiatives shows why we need to focus our attention on areas such as education and training if we are to see meaningful progress in preventing violations of IHL against protected persons. As the Cold War sputtered to an end in the late 1980s and early 1990s, hopes were raised among many for a period of relative peace across the world. Unfortunately, the atrocities in the wars of Yugoslavian secession beginning in 1991 and the genocide of the Tutsi by their Hutu fellow citizens in Rwanda in 1994 soon showed that the tragedies of armed conflict upon civilians and detainees were not going away. This reality led to two important developments at the international level—the creation of the standing International Criminal Court pursuant to the Rome Statute of 1998[17] and the development of the norm of the Responsibility to Protect.

The International Criminal Court

Building on the work performed by the International Criminal Tribunal for the Former Yugoslavia and the International Criminal Tribunal for Rwanda,[18] the International Criminal Court was given jurisdiction to try cases of genocide, crimes against humanity, war crimes, and the crime of aggression (as eventually defined).[19] Expectations as to its potential impact on protecting victims of these crimes were very high.[20] Since it began in 2002, it has held some key trials that have established important precedents in the modern application and enforcement of IHL. One of the latest of these cases is that of the Congolese rebel leader Bosco Ntaganda for crimes against humanity and war crimes, including murder, sexual slavery, and the conscription of child soldiers, which resulted in a 30-year sentence.[21]

The court's work has faced several challenges, however. First, its output has been quite limited. As of late 2019, trials before the court had resulted in only nine convictions, but four acquittals.[22] Second, its work has been hampered since its inception by political opposition from countries including the United States,[23] and a perception that it is being used to primarily try African defendants[24] while avoiding those from more powerful countries. Unfortunately, even its advocates recognize that the court's performance in authorizing investigations and issuing opinions is subpar, and that it has struggled "to inform and meet victim expectations."[25]

The Responsibility to Protect

Likewise prompted by the tragedies of Rwanda and the Serb massacre of Bosniak civilians at Srebrenica,[26] the Responsibility to Protect concept was first formulated by the International Commission on Intervention and State Sovereignty in 2001.[27] At its heart, the Responsibility to Protect recognized that nations had the task of ensuring that their people were protected by preventing conflict, by reacting to conflict situations appropriately, and by rebuilding and seeking reconciliation afterwards. Importantly, it also held that appropriate collective reactions to conflict situations would include "in extreme cases military intervention."[28] These principles gained some traction and were later affirmed by heads of state and government in the 2005 World Summit Outcome Document, which was adopted by the General Assembly.[29]

Implementation, however, proved difficult. The 2001 report assumed an overly optimistic set of conditions under which military intervention would be conducted with the minimum use of force.[30] Although the UN Security Council's 2011 resolution allowing members to become involved in protecting Libyan dissidents from the Libyan government contained language that reflected the Responsibility to Protect,[31] in the end what became a largely NATO-led operation struck some as a means to accomplish regime change through the pretext of a humanitarian mission.[32] When the civil war in Syria escalated to the point of the Assad regime gassing its own people in 2013, China's and Russia's opposition to meaningful UN Security Council action and the Obama administration's lack of resolution in taking military action outside an authorization from the council likely marked the end of practical implementation of the Responsibility to Protect in its most potent form,[33] other than in certain peacekeeping operations perhaps.[34]

The work of the International Criminal Court and the implementation of the norm of the Responsibility to Protect have largely not met the high goals their proponents had expected of them. However, they do represent progress toward greater appreciation for the role that the protection of civilians and detainees should play in the conduct of armed conflicts by combatant actors. From the perspective of those who suffer serious violations of IHL, though, one of the main problems with these efforts is not that the somewhat lofty expectations of these initiatives matched poorly with international political reality. The larger problem is probably that both mechanisms come into play too late in the course of human rights violations to avoid often irreparable consequences to the lives, dignity, and property of detainees and innocent civilians.[35]

The possible deterrence value of potential international prosecution[36] or military intervention sanctioned by the United Nations likely matters little to combatants who are actively violating IHL in real time. That is why we should revisit the international legal duties that militaries have to educate and train their troops in IHL and find better ways to make that instruction more effective in avoiding violations against civilians and detainees from the start. This must include a greater emphasis on values as an effective backstop for IHL compliance. As Rossi has cogently noted regarding the importance of including basic values in IHL training rather than just emphasizing the legal norms:

> Indeed, the aim of effective IHL training is not to provide armed forces with the skills needed to analyse or justify military action from a legal perspective. It must enable them to fully identify what IHL prescribes as the "right thing to do"—and then do it.[37]

IHL Education and Training and the Effects of IHL Violations

Since the Al Qaeda terrorist attacks in the northeastern United States in 2001, there have been tragic instances of IHL violations in the conflicts Western nations and their coalition partners have fought. These include the abuse of detainees by US forces in Afghanistan[38] and Iraq[39] and the purposeful targeting and murder of civilians by certain troops.[40] These crimes undermined the coalitions' larger messages of following the rule of law and respecting human rights.

In addition to the ethical and legal issues raised by such events, conducting military operations in compliance with IHL can be crucial to maintaining continued public support for missions in the host nations that are likely bearing the brunt of any combat. For example, in a poll of Iraqis conducted in May 2004 after the mistreatment of detainees at Abu Ghraib had become public, over half stated that they believed that this was the way that all Americans behaved. Not surprisingly, 92 percent saw the coalition forces led by the United States as occupiers, as compared to the 2 percent who viewed them as liberators, and 86 percent wanted them to leave Iraq at once when a new Iraqi government had been elected.[41]

IHL violations put governments immediately on the defensive, as they try to explain to domestic and international audiences that these are unfortunate aberrations that do not reflect the disciplined and law-compliant nature of their armed forces overall.[42] Certain countries such as Australia[43] and Canada[44] have taken the very serious step of disbanding entire units in response to severe IHL violations. Generally speaking, additional training has always been a common remedy in militaries for troops that have significant problems in meeting accepted standards. Importantly however, IHL violations have continued to occur despite the education and training efforts of the coalition forces to comply with their respective nations' international legal obligations under IHL to provide information about this body of law to their troops and to educate and train them on it. Simply requiring more IHL training is not the answer.

As to standards, there can be no acceptable level of IHL violations. By the same token, though, it is not easy at this time to quantitatively establish how effective IHL education and training is in preventing them.[45] Literature regarding measures of performance abounds, such as training frequency, the different types of training given, and the educational and training curricula that are available in different languages to teach troops from different countries.[46] Measures of effectiveness, on the other hand, such as the calibration of training methods, the degree to which soldiers retain the information they receive during training and are able to apply it in actual field work, and the steps to identify and remediate training deficiencies, are much less common.

This shortcoming in IHL education and training could be effectively addressed by coupling the existing work of nations and of the ICRC in providing information about IHL, IHL instruction, and instructional resources to the global community with a more quantitatively critical approach to IHL training effectiveness. Further, this approach should also promote meaningful engagement with soldiers on positive military values rather than just legal norms. The goal should be the building of moral reasoning skills in all officers and soldiers from a systemic perspective of resilience, so that regardless of how tired, how hungry, or how angry soldiers might be over injuries or deaths sustained by their comrades, there is always a base setting of moral reasoning that will help keep them compliant with IHL.

Outline of the Chapters

In each of the chapters, I will describe and examine in detail the different case studies and approaches used by the educators, trainers, and researchers in delivering IHL and IHL-related instruction. After setting out the factual background, I will then analyze the results of these case studies and their approaches and link these to steps that could be taken by IHL instructors in general to make their programs more effective, and to measure whether this is being accomplished. Finally, I will summarize the primary lessons that I drew from these studies.

Chapter 1

In Chapter 1, I will first review work that has been done by the ICRC over the past 20 years that has used data to first move its efforts from simply disseminating information about IHL toward working with militaries to integrate IHL principles and practice throughout their intellectual infrastructure. Importantly, this work is now driving an evolution from integration to internalization, a recognition that effective IHL education and training likely requires troops to see how IHL concepts and principles complement and reinforce shared values and standards related to a professional and personal military ethic. This chapter will examine how this shift has led to a greater understanding of the use of data to arrive at more sound conclusions as to what is actually effective in promoting IHL compliance in different militaries. Importantly, these conclusions suggest that traditional means and methods of teaching and training IHL need to be critically reexamined.

These are the primary lessons I draw from studying this evolution:

- Particularly in liberal democracies where military establishments are under effective civilian control, troops are not drained of the moral values with which they were raised or the moral reasoning skills they developed as they grew up in their families and communities. The discipline instilled in them through realistic training, military authority, and the bonds they form with their comrades do not eliminate their ability to exercise these values or to reason morally.
- Consistent with this agency, compliance with IHL by an individual soldier can be fostered through military socialization, which leads that soldier to internalize IHL principles as an aspect of a positive and collective professional military identity.
- Leaders' values matter to those whom they lead. Depending upon national and military culture, different leaders at different levels will have the greatest influence on soldiers internalizing what is right and what is wrong regarding their treatment of civilians and detainees.
- While the language of the law might be universal, by itself in the abstract it likely has only modest meaning for most soldiers in their everyday work. When IHL principles are coupled with values that register both emotionally

and cognitively with soldiers, however, the likelihood that they will comply with them grows.

- There is a growing international crisis of doubt in the efficacy of IHL to protect those who are not in combat. Traditional methods and approaches to IHL instruction do not appear to be up to the task of restoring trust in this crucial area of the law.

Chapter 2

If only because of the sheer number of troops the United States has deployed abroad since 2001, and the extent of the regulatory, doctrinal, and training infrastructure that supports them, Chapters 2, 3, and 4 will focus largely on US efforts to gather and analyze data relevant to IHL training effectiveness.

In Chapter 2, I will start exploring this data by looking at the results of a previously unpublished survey that was made of new field-grade officers in combat and combat support branches who were students at the US Army Command & General Staff College (CGSC) when the 2001 Al Qaeda attacks occurred. Although certain survey design flaws and the lack of a follow-up survey of these officers limit the usefulness of the results, the survey answers provide a historical snapshot of attitudes and experiences regarding IHL education and training at a particularly crucial time. These students had relatively recently been company-grade commanders, and their former troops and the successor commanders they left in charge of their units were likely among those deployed first into Afghanistan and then shortly thereafter into Iraq.

These are the primary lessons I draw from considering these survey results:

- The use of role players in training exercises is a very effective form of instruction delivery, particularly for junior soldiers. This more realistically presents soldiers with the environments they will find themselves working in once they deploy, and role players also make the instruction less abstract in terms of applying IHL principles to situations with actual people.
- Soldiers need more tangible reasons to follow IHL other than it is the law, and if they follow it, their adversaries might reciprocate. Depending on an adversary's behavior to foster your own troops' compliance with IHL is not a good idea—reasons for compliance must instead be within the control of their leaders and themselves.
- Even within a specific military service, there will likely be differences in how different service branches best engage with IHL education and training. For example, what works with conventional soldiers might not work well with special forces troops.

- Case study discussion or seminar-style IHL training should be used more frequently with junior officers, and it should also be used with NCOs rather than the lecture presentations that appear to be more common.
- There are certain times in soldiers' careers when it is likely most efficient to harvest data regarding their experiences and impressions regarding IHL and IHL-related training. For young officers, one of those times is likely the transition from company- to field-grade rank, from being small-unit commanders to becoming new staff officers.
- Similarly, junior officers are likely an underserved group in terms of IHL education and training. Increased investment in these young commanders who are closest to their troops would likely yield dividends in IHL compliance by their subordinates throughout the course of their careers.

Chapter 3

In Chapter 3, I will explore surveys that captured what US troops experienced physically and psychologically during their deployments to Afghanistan and Iraq between 2006 and 2007. These surveys were primarily designed to assess the mental health status of the troops during times of particularly intense combat in those two countries. From a command perspective, these surveys would have been worthwhile if they had only led to a better understanding of what was impacting the troops' mental health and the potential relationships between these factors and their behavior in the field during combat operations. But the survey teams went further.

Originally at the request of a senior commander in Iraq in 2006, and then apparently with at least the tacit approval of commanders in Afghanistan and Iraq in 2007, these surveys included questions that specifically addressed the troops' attitudes and behaviors regarding what the surveys termed unethical conduct—conduct that international lawyers would recognize as being inconsistent with IHL. The surveys included questions about what the troops thought of their training, whether their own behavior was IHL-compliant, and the likelihood that they would report their comrades for certain acts that would violate IHL. Asking combat soldiers who were still engaged in combat these sorts of questions was unprecedented, and the survey results provide a valuable window into the actual attitudes and behaviors of troops related to IHL when they are applying it in the field.

These are the primary lessons I draw from examining these survey results:

- Asking soldiers who are in combat about their perceptions, attitudes, and behaviors regarding IHL within the context of a medical survey rather than directly asking about their compliance with IHL is more likely to elicit honest responses.

- Because of the strong bonds between comrades in small units, when presented with a hypothetical situation, most soldiers surveyed in a combat theater would apparently not report their colleagues for violations of IHL. However, the vast majority of these same soldiers did not report having committed even relatively minor IHL infractions. This shows there is a reservoir of self-discipline that can be tapped in seeking to internalize IHL principles in the average soldier.
- Soldiers' mental well-being has direct and indirect impacts on their perceptions, attitudes, and behaviors regarding IHL. Repeated combat deployments, the degree of combat exposure, and lack of sleep are risk factors in maintaining soldiers' mental health. High-quality leadership, from both officers and NCOs, is a protective factor.

Chapter 4

I will start Chapter 4 describing how in Iraq the survey results drove the development of a data-driven, multidisciplinary military ethics and IHL training program for US troops in a multinational division. This program was taught by leaders at all levels between late 2007 and early 2008. Surveys conducted a couple months after the training program showed statistically significant improvements in metrics related to the troops' IHL compliance. The construction, content, and delivery of this training program and the results of this instruction will be reviewed in detail.

This chapter will also review how, shortly before the 2007 surveys were conducted, the US Army had responded to the debacle of Abu Ghraib's IHL violations by instituting an IHL training program that emphasized the role of military attorneys as IHL instructors and focused largely on the delivery of the legal norms of IHL instruction. Meaningful empirical assessment of the training's effectiveness does not appear to have been a significant part of this program at the beginning, nor does it appear to be part of it today. This chapter will conclude with an examination of American legal scholarship on empiricism and IHL compliance and what these approaches might mean for the assessment of IHL training effectiveness.

These are the primary lessons I draw from examining the battlefield ethics training program, the current US Army approach to IHL and IHL-related education and training, and scholarly work focused on the assessment of IHL education and training efficacy within the US IHL compliance construct:

- The battlefield ethics training program shows that a multidisciplinary team, armed with command support and specific data, can quickly and cheaply develop an effective IHL training program, the results of which can be measured even in a combat theater. Lawyers do not need to be in charge of these sorts of efforts.
- Mental health issues in general were not strongly associated with IHL violations, although particular types were, including feelings of rage. The strongest predictor of behaviors such as maltreatment of civilians or detainees was instead the level of combat exposure experienced by the soldiers. The greater the level of combat exposure the more likely a given soldier is to have experienced the injury or death of a comrade, or even injury to themselves, which might lead to anger and rage.
- Leaders talking to their subordinates about the IHL compliance issues they face and how they might address them matters a great deal to the led.
- It is consistent with IHL treaties to make lawyers the proponents in a military organization for IHL training. It is not necessarily the most effective approach, however, and whether it is effective can be determined through measurement.
- Merely linking IHL principles with official military values in doctrinal documents is not sufficient to create the education and training products and programs necessary to effectively instruct soldiers in either.
- In a law-heavy IHL compliance construct, there are inherent difficulties in using empirical assessment of results such as investigation reports and military discipline findings to determine the efficacy of IHL education and training. Further, such efforts are subject to politicization. The better approach is to focus on preventing violations rather than relying on their adjudication afterwards.

Chapter 5

In Chapter 5, I will return to IHL education and training in academic, training, and garrison settings and look at some examples of work that has been done in the past decade that incorporates data collection and analysis in the delivery of IHL and IHL-related instruction. These programs include an experiment with Norwegian cadets that assessed their ability to resolve moral dilemmas in a state of sleep deprivation, a moral decision-making course taught to young Swiss officers, a basic IHL course taught to new Malian troops as they trained for combat deployment, and a case study of a leadership development program conducted by a US Army battalion in Germany. With an eye to the future of IHL training and the need to leverage technology and young troops' technological savviness, this chapter will finish with an assessment of two case studies involving university students, the first in Northern Ireland and the second in Japan, that used war video games as an IHL teaching tool.

These are the primary lessons I draw from reviewing these very different case studies and, in certain instances, interviewing their authors:

- Building moral reasoning resilience in soldiers requires a layered and systematic approach to understanding how it actually works in tired and anxious minds. An important goal should be the development of a default moral reasoning methodology that can endure being degraded by combat conditions of sleeplessness and fear.
- Efficient problem solving is a hallmark of typical military reasoning skills. These skills, however, do not translate well to developing moral reasoning abilities. IHL and IHL-related education and training requires specialized instructional approaches to develop these abilities.
- Austere training environments and modest budgets are no excuse for not developing holistic IHL training programs that include data collection and analysis to assess their efficacy and which are tailored to the experiences and values of the training audiences.
- Although training IHL under realistic conditions of stress can likely make a significant impression on soldiers, the moral intensity of training can itself generate useful emotional responses. For example, visiting historical sites of atrocities against civilians and detainees can result in memorable learning even though there is no physical stress.
- Information technology holds tremendous promise in providing interesting and realistic IHL training for young soldiers, in media they enjoy using, such as simulations or so-called first-person shooter war video games. However, there are IHL application and ethical concerns that will need to be addressed through focused research before we immediately jump to using these tools on a large scale.

Conclusion

In closing, I will address the cross-cutting themes that I have found regarding the use of data to drive more effective IHL training in looking at these different approaches in the case studies. Although some of the studies are narrow in focus, and sometimes small in terms of their sample sizes, an analysis of their approaches reveals important points that are generally applicable across the range of IHL educational and training programs. Further, they provide important launch points for additional research and study in making IHL instruction more effective.

We must recognize that approaches driven by data will likely always need to be iterative and, to a degree, experimental. Not all experiments are successful, but the objective lessons we learn from them can move us closer to success the next time. We must seek practical solutions and acknowledge from the beginning that we are not likely to ever achieve complete perfection in terms of our soldiers not committing IHL violations against civilians and detainees.

I will also address the need to focus IHL education and training more on young leaders, both officers and NCOs, and to move them to the front in instruction for their troops. To properly support these leaders, we do not need more lawyers. Instead, we need to develop multidisciplinary approaches that involve fellow professionals skilled in ethics, psychology, statistics, and curriculum development and delivery. Consistent with a multidisciplinary approach, values need to become an integral part of IHL and IHL-related training.

Finally, we need to systematically fashion our curricula and data collection and analysis plans to fit our specific audiences and the particular needs of the students and trainees in our classes. This includes the need to provide feedback both to the troops whom we are instructing and to the systems we are using to instruct them. Although I believe these steps can be done in affordable and sustainable ways, I will also identify what I see as potential challenges to implementing this sort of approach at the international, national, and military service levels and even within different units in a particular military service.

With that as a backdrop, let us begin by exploring the role of data and the consideration of values over the past 20 years in driving the ICRC's evolving approach to enhancing IHL compliance.

Chapter 1

ICRC'S EVOLVING APPROACH TO IHL TRAINING

Since its founding in 1863, the ICRC has grown to become the preeminent organization internationally in matters involving IHL.[1] The fundamental work it performed in bringing the international community together to negotiate the 1949 Geneva Conventions and the Additional Protocols in 1977, coupled with its wide ranging field work promoting the protection of victims of armed conflict and the understanding of IHL,[2] gives it unrivaled authority in this area. Consistent with the roles set out for it under these treaties and in its own statutes,[3] for many years the ICRC's engagement with armed forces placed a heavy emphasis on the dissemination of IHL texts and the teaching of IHL.[4]

Unfortunately, despite diligent engagement and instruction efforts by the ICRC, IHL violations continued to occur in armed conflict. Over the past two decades, as researchers and writers affiliated with the ICRC sought to find ways to make IHL training more effective and to promote greater compliance by military personnel, they have increasingly begun using empirical approaches to address this problem. Over time, this continued examination of IHL instruction effectiveness has increasingly recognized the significance of leadership, unit cohesion, and professional identity and values in fostering soldiers' compliance with IHL—rather than just expecting troops to follow IHL because it is the law.

A Holistic Worldwide Assessment: The First "People on War" Report

To commemorate the 50th anniversary of the 1949 Geneva Conventions, the ICRC commissioned a comprehensive worldwide survey of public attitudes toward IHL and its application in armed conflict. The survey's results were published in 1999, and the survey included participants from 12 countries that had fairly recently experienced armed conflict within their borders, as well as people from the countries that were permanent members of the UN Security Council (with the exception of the People's Republic of China). People from

Switzerland were also surveyed. Although the surveys were not geared toward assessing impressions and experiences with IHL training in particular, and the respondents were a mix of civilians and combatants,[5] some of the results are very helpful in setting the context that contemporary IHL instructors need to understand in creating and delivering effective IHL curricula today.

Why do troops attack or hurt civilians?

When asked to choose two reasons that they believed best explained why troops attacked or hurt civilians, 30 percent of the respondents from the countries that had recently experienced armed conflict believed it was because the troops wanted to win at any cost. Twenty-seven percent said that it was because the troops were indifferent to IHL. Twenty-six percent said it was because troops hated their enemy, and 24 percent said that it was because the troops had been ordered to do so. Only 14 percent believed that it was because the troops were not aware of the law.[6]

One set of questions addressed "circularity," that is, the impact that being injured in an armed conflict had upon respondents' attitudes toward taking, or refraining from, certain actions against protected persons under IHL. For example, the first question in this set asked respondents whether they agreed with two statements: first, that it was "okay to attack civilians who voluntarily give food and shelter to enemy combatants," and second, that this was not permissible. Among those who identified as lacking any combat experience, 22 percent believed this IHL violation was acceptable, and 75 percent did not. Among those who identified as combatants, 32 percent found such attacks were permissible, and 65 percent did not. These results were largely the same for each of the other three questions.[7]

The respondents' answers were also separated out on the basis of specific war experiences, whether their relatives had been killed, whether they had been imprisoned, whether they knew someone who had been raped, and whether they had been wounded. The responses here were consistent as well. Slightly less than a third of the respondents agreed that the actions against civilians were acceptable, and the remainder did not. From this, the report concluded that "an embittering war experience intensifies the threat to the barriers protecting civilians."[8] It is doubtful that experiencing armed conflict in any fashion is a positive thing for most people, but these findings suggest that it is particular negative experiences, specifically traumatic events, that have the greatest impact on whether people believe that they should follow IHL in general.

The origin of the norm of civilian protection

Respondents were also asked to identify the primary basis for the norm that it was wrong to attack civilians. The responses revealed important differences between respondents from UN Security Council permanent members and those from nations that had recently experienced armed conflict.

For example, the British and American respondents were similar in that few believed that the norm was rooted in their culture: 3 and 5 percent, respectively. But where the percentages of Britons who believed that the primary bases of the norm were law or religion were very similar, 8 and 9 percent, respectively, twice as many Americans found religion to be the primary basis as compared to the law, 26 versus 12 percent. In contrast to both the Americans and the Britons, about 80 percent of the respondents who were Afghan or Palestinian identified religion as the primary basis for the norm.

As to Americans generally and religion, it is useful to note that religious identification among them has decreased markedly since this survey was taken, with the number of people reporting no religious preference increasing from 8 percent in 1999 to 21 percent in 2019.[9] These findings suggest that IHL curriculum developers and instructors need to consider not only the impact that religion might have on specific training audiences' attitudes and IHL-compliant behaviors but also how these impacts might change over time. Conversely, emphasizing international law as the basis for the norm seems unlikely to register in a meaningful way among many students of IHL instruction irrespective of their country of origin and its culture.

Finally, while human rights were noted by roughly half of all respondents as the most common basis for the norm, 43 percent of those from UN Security Council permanent members and 31 percent from the 12 countries that had recently experienced armed conflict identified their own personal code as the norm's primary basis.[10] If this trend holds true today, contemporary IHL instructors and trainers need to take account of the role of individual ethical identities in finding ways to make IHL education and training more effective. Obviously, it is not practicable for instructors to identify each individual student's or soldier's ethical code and then tailor instruction precisely to address them from a resource perspective, and military commanders are unlikely to view this as either necessary or desirable given their expectations of standard and uniform responses from all their troops. These findings do suggest, however, that the aspects of IHL that people are willing to internalize, and to incorporate into their personal ethical identity (even if it springs from a shared group identity), could be very helpful in avoiding violations of IHL.

An Empirical Assessment of the Sources of Behavior in Armed Conflict

The "People on War" report was part of the basis for a 2004 ICRC study on IHL training effectiveness that was likewise driven by data. In this study, "The Roots of Behaviour in War," the researchers conducted surveys of approximately one hundred current and former combatants in each of the four countries that they evaluated as significantly impacted by armed conflict: Bosnia-Herzegovina, Colombia, the Republic of the Congo, and Georgia.[11] Although many of their findings were not surprising, it is important that their conclusions were confirmed with data. For example, the researchers found an understanding of IHL principles to be universal, and that although adherence to these norms did not guarantee IHL-compliant behavior, following these norms did help "people to resist negative dynamics which would lock them into spirals of violence."[12] Consistent with the "People on War" report upon which a significant amount of their research was based, the researchers also assessed that "combatants who have taken part in hostilities, and been subjected to humiliation and trauma are led, in the short term, to perpetrate violations of IHL."[13]

The conflict between legal norms and attitudes shaped by military authority

In describing the characteristics that combatants tended to share, the researchers found that because of the peer pressure to which soldiers were subjected, they experienced "depersonalization, loss of independence, and a high degree of conformity." They noted the strong bonds that often form between combatants, and that allegiance to the group and submission to superior military authority promoted "the dilution of the individual responsibility of the combatant within the collective responsibility of his combat unit." In their view, the individual soldier was "rendered even more docile by military training and collective preparation for confrontation with an enemy that is often demonized and dehumanized."[14]

In this context, the researchers found that the occurrence of IHL violations (despite acknowledged understanding of IHL's basic principles among combatants) sprang from the "moral disengagement" caused by resorting to victim-based justifications for the violence based on the combatants' traumatic experiences and dehumanization of their enemies.[15] This potentially set up significant ethical dilemmas for soldiers as they decided whether to follow the law or the orders of their leaders and the inclinations of their comrades. This tension acted to undermine their compliance with IHL despite their training.[16]

As a result of their research, the authors of "The Roots of Behavior in War" came to two primary conclusions, which in hindsight probably should have been treated with a greater degree of skepticism than they appear to have been at the time. First, the authors concluded that training soldiers on IHL needed to be a "legal and political matter rather than a moral one, and focus more on norms than their underlying values." This was because in their view, values were vague and relativistic, and the "idea that that combatant is morally autonomous is mistaken." Second, soldiers would only comply more with IHL when "they are under strict orders as to the conduct to adopt and if effective sanctions are applied in the event they fail to obey such orders."[17] One might assess that the researchers appear to have viewed soldiers largely as automatons without independent moral agency, who needed first to be properly programmed and then appropriately punished when they acted outside their programming.

In fairness to the authors' conclusions, there is no doubt that there are extremely negative examples of commanders directly ordering soldiers to shoot people whom neither the commanders nor the soldiers had a good-faith basis to believe were combatants. For example, a US Army lieutenant was convicted of murder in 2013 for compelling his soldiers to follow his orders and kill two Afghan civilians who gave no sign of participating in combat at the time they were engaged.[18] There are instances of soldiers exhibiting moral disengagement by killing civilians essentially for sport, such as a US Army sergeant who was convicted in 2011 for the murder of three Afghan civilians as part of a so-called kill squad.[19] Finally, there are certainly instances of soldiers succumbing to toxic peer pressure to commit IHL violations. An example of this is the allegations made against certain Australian special forces NCOs, who apparently required junior soldiers to kill Afghan detainees as a rite of initiation into the unit.[20]

Although these tragic events justify a critical examination of IHL training and compliance even in generally well-disciplined armed forces, they are much more the exception than the rule in both the Australian and US militaries. In this sense, "The Roots of Behaviour in War" study paints with far too broad a brush in assessing the lack of moral agency among soldiers. As Mastroanni has noted, such a conclusion largely devalues the meaningful influence that positive moral decision-making and the values that go along with it could exert through leaders manifesting this in their actions. This approach largely ignores soldiers' individual moral responsibility for their decisions, potentially reducing them to being viewed as "automatons or puppets unable to control themselves in the face of 'situational pressures.'"[21] It also ignores how useful peer pressure to conform to a shared ethic of professionalism consistent with IHL could be.

Assessing the study's conclusions

"The Roots of Behaviour in War" study had a very significant influence on the direction that the ICRC's interaction with militaries would then take, and it led to the development of what became known as the "integration approach." Under this approach, the ICRC sought to work with governments and militaries to further embed IHL norms throughout military doctrine, education and training, equipment, and sanctions.[22] These were important steps and doubtlessly furthered the ICRC's mission to disseminate information about IHL and to increase awareness of it. From the perspective of data, however, it is not clear why the ICRC believed that this approach alone would achieve anything more than an incremental increase in IHL compliance.

First, although "The Roots of Behaviour in War" researchers surveyed approximately four hundred people with combat experience, the quantitative results of these surveys are neither reproduced nor discussed in detail in the article describing the study. That makes it difficult to test their conclusions on the basis of their research and to see whether the data might support other conclusions than the ones they drew. Unlike the "People on War" report, their article does not contain a complete description of the questions asked by the survey instrument, so it is difficult to assess whether there were instances of potential ambiguity or bias in the questions.

Second, despite relying on the data from the "People on War" report, the study's authors appear to have disregarded information in the report that suggested that values were very important in determining how respondents in different cultures and different countries understood the general IHL norms and whether the respondents would comply with IHL. In addition, relatively few respondents in the "People on War" report relied on the notion that the law itself was the basis for the norm of not attacking civilians. This casts further doubt on the conclusion in "The Roots of Behaviour in War" study that focusing just on the legal norms was the best approach to increasing compliance with IHL.

The ICRC's New "Culture of Restraint" Approach

Over time, IHL violations continued to occur despite the increasing embedding of IHL principles and content into the doctrine and manuals of different national militaries, and legal writers began to reassess the findings and recommendations made by the authors of "The Roots of Behaviour in War" study. For example, as early as 2008, Castano, Leidner, and Slawuta emphasized the importance of factoring small group dynamics within military units and individual soldiers' perceptions of themselves into efforts to ensure

IHL compliance. While acknowledging the importance of continuing work to disseminate information about IHL and to incorporate it into training, they concluded that this needed to be done

> with an eye to making respect for certain norms central to the soldier's identity (as opposed to an afterthought), and ensuring that military units, particularly when engaged in violent combat, do not become psychologically isolated from the larger entities of which they are part.[23]

In a particularly sound critique of "The Roots of Behaviour in War" study in 2014, Stephens questioned the study's authors' heavy reliance on the normative integrity of the law to foster compliance. He also was skeptical of their emphasis on moral neutrality, since it came at the cost of appreciating how the internalization by individuals of basic IHL values could also contribute to IHL compliance.[24] Stephens noted that in reality many important aspects of the applicable law were not quite as settled as the study's authors appeared to believe they were, and that "moreover, marginalizing any kind of moral or social content that might underpin the [interpretation of IHL] surrenders enormous authority to lawyers and the legal process."[25]

"The Roots of Restraint in War" study

In 2018, the ICRC revisited "The Roots of Behaviour in War" study's findings and, in a new report, "The Roots of Restraint in War," came to markedly different conclusions as to how IHL training could be done most effectively. This new study noted how influential "The Roots of Behaviour in War" report had been in realigning the ICRC's approach to IHL compliance, shifting its focus from informing militaries and armed groups on the content of IHL to "pursuing more robust efforts to ensure that the legal framework was incorporated into the inner workings" of these organizations. However, based on the results of large-scale surveys and interviews of soldiers from different types of armed organizations, including surveys of 409 Australian and 1,030 Filipino soldiers it had conducted, the new study recognized that this was not enough. In addition to these efforts, the researchers concluded that "we can do better by understanding how a culture of restraint is socialized, not only formally and vertically, from the top down, but also informally and horizontally."[26]

"The Roots of Restraint in War" study found that for both the Australian and Filipino soldiers, more intensive training resulted in "greater adoption of norms of restraint by combatants," as did more intense training. For example, it noted that the Australian Royal Military College had conducted a week-long training exercise with cadets that purposefully deprived them of food and sleep. During the exercise, instructors sought to persuade the cadets to engage in "simulated unethical and unlawful behavior," and a significant number of cadets did so. The instructors then anonymized recordings of the cadets' actions and replayed them for the cadets in a classroom setting. Feedback from the cadets indicated that they were shocked by what had happened, and that this experience more than anything had convinced them "of the need to develop a strong moral compass before facing the stress of the battlefield."[27]

The surveys of the Australian and Filipino soldiers also suggested that the credibility of the instructor with the training audience was very important. For both, "an effective instructor in IHL require[d] credibility derived from operational experience: they need to be able to draw on the dilemmas they have faced and explain the choices they made." Military legal advisors were not rated highly by either group of soldiers, because they found these officers "to be generalists from higher echelons with no direct combat experience." But where the Australian troops found instructors with actual military experience in armed conflict to be more credible, their Filipino counterparts were more comfortable with an experienced civilian instructor.[28]

Army personnel from these two countries also assessed the risk of punishment under IHL as much less significant to their decision-making than the possibility of punishment under domestic and military law, but this risk was more significant to officers than it was to enlisted soldiers. However, what mattered most was the socializing effect of informal norms and "army values." Soldiers recognized that the influence of these factors as expressed in the sense of unit cohesion and bonds between comrades was amplified, for example, by the decentralized nature of counterinsurgency warfare. Perhaps foreshadowing the 2020 Brereton Report on IHL violations by an Australian special forces squadron,[29] they also recognized that these influences were particularly pronounced in special operations units, which often operate very autonomously.[30] This evidences a great deal of variation and complexity in the understanding of normative standards among individuals in different military organizations, which further calls into question the effectiveness of the recommended approach in "The Roots of Behaviour in War" study.

As an example of this complexity, this study related the results of a survey experiment involving Australian Army officers and enlisted soldiers. Participants were presented with one of four different scenarios involving a proposed attack on an important target in a residential area. In the control scenario, the participants were only informed that there would be civilian casualties. The next scenario included the additional element of the unit's legal advisor's assessment that the attack would violate IHL. The third scenario included the additional element that a majority of unit members believed that the attack was unethical. The fourth scenario added both the legal advisor's assessment and the opinion of the unit. The participants were then asked the degree to which they agreed or disagreed that the planned attack would be proper.[31]

Interestingly, the officers' decisions on whether to attack were more influenced by both the legal advisor's assessment and the unit sense of the attack than were the enlisted soldiers' decisions, and the greatest impact on the officers' decision-making occurred when presented with both pieces of information.[32] The study did not provide an explanation for this rank-differentiated difference. However, it is a data point to keep in mind when thinking about the positive role of junior NCOs as well as commanders in setting the example for their troops in ethical decision-making.

Different armies; different leadership influence realities

The results of this experiment suggest that the officers were weighing and incorporating different ethical perspectives into their decision-making than were the enlisted soldiers—perhaps a more holistic approach to resolving IHL questions. These results are particularly important when considering whose example soldiers would prefer to follow in this regard. In a more granular examination of data collected during this study that was published in 2021, researchers involved in this effort conducted a specific survey of 243 Australian Army and 546 Filipino Army personnel that tested their relative preferences among military advantage, force protection, and civilian protection. The respondents included battalion commanders, junior NCOs, and enlisted soldiers.[33]

For example, researchers explored the tension between force protection and civilian protection in the decision-making of the respondents by presenting them with the statement, "During combat operations, it is justifiable to kill a civilian if it will save the life of a soldier." The respondents then indicated their degree of concurrence with the statement by selecting a value on a five-point scale, ranging from "1" for strong agreement to "5" for strong disagreement. The differences between the respondents from the two armies were striking.[34]

In their responses to the question that tested their preferences between protection of civilians and military advantage, there was a statistically significant difference between the senior Australian Army officers' responses and the enlisted soldiers' responses, with the officers more strongly favoring civilian protection over military advantage. In their responses to the question comparing force protection and protection of civilians, the differences were even more pronounced. The battalion commanders prioritized civilian protection, while the junior enlisted soldiers markedly favored force protection.

In fact, the results showed that across all three survey questions, the officers' preference for civilian protection was stronger than those of both the junior NCOs and the junior enlisted soldiers.[35]

Some might say this is only logical, because the battalion commanders were probably much less likely to have people shooting at them during an operation. In contrast, however, the Filipino officers and junior soldiers both reported "consistently high levels of norm adoption." In fact, "junior enlisted report[ed] slightly higher levels of norm adoption than senior officers: across all three measures, junior soldiers [were] even more emphatic in their prioritization of civilian protection norms than their senior officers."[36]

Important differences between the Australian and Filipino junior enlisted soldiers were shown in their responses to the survey question that asked them to rank unit factors that had influenced their views on the proper treatment of civilians in armed conflict. The Australian soldiers ranked their junior NCOs and their platoon mates as being significantly more influential than their senior officers. The responses of the Filipino soldiers were more mixed, finding their battalion commanders as "having somewhat greater influence [...] than platoon sergeants [...] or other junior enlisted platoon members." The results of follow-up focus group sessions and interviews of respondents confirmed these findings.[37]

The researchers came to three conclusions. First, "the adoption of organizational norms is not necessarily uniform across salient subgroups within military organizations." This suggests the need to take a tailored approach to different units in teaching and training IHL. Second, within different militaries, correlations between rank and norm adoption will not be the same.[38] This suggests that even within certain units, different rank cohorts may need different instruction for it to be most effective. It is important to note that this is not the same as recognizing that different ranks likely need different instruction based of their relative levels of command or leadership responsibility—that is not a new concept.[39] These findings go deeper and indicate that different ranks will often have different degrees of norm uptake and internalization.

Third, in what the researchers called the "paradox of rank," depending on the military, the leaders who have the most influence on the junior enlisted soldiers might be those with the least formal command authority, such as the junior NCOs. This suggests that an empirical analysis of actual influence vectors in a military organization, coupled with an assessment of the attitudes of those vectors toward the norms commanders and instructors are seeking to instill among soldiers, could identify areas where IHL education and training efforts require different training strategies.[40] If commanders really want to set the example for all of their troops, an effective way to accomplish this might be to specifically engage with their junior sergeants and corporals to talk about their ethical decision models.

Features of a holistic and systematic IHL training program

"The Roots of Restraint in War" study found that both armies seemed to have taken what it assessed as a hybrid approach in melding aspects of informal socialization with formal norms and the creation of "army values" that emphasized a common set of ethical principles for all military members. These values appealed to the soldiers' sense of professionalism and personal honor and created a sense of military identity. The researchers concluded that inculcating these values among soldiers was more effective in fostering IHL compliance than relying on enforcement mechanisms alone. Thus, there was "a need for both the law and the values underpinning it, with the emphasis of each influence dependent on the target audience." The researchers also assessed that reliance on these values could help convince soldiers to continue to comply with IHL even when their enemies did not.[41]

The researchers concluded that the intensity of training in IHL, as a function of how often it is given and the use of tailored instructional methods, leads to different outcomes in terms of soldiers' conduct in operations. Mixed training methods that combined IHL briefings, classroom discussions, case study reviews, and practical exercises in the field appeared to be most effective. Trainers must be found credible by troops, and training audiences appeared to prefer receiving instruction from trainers who had themselves experienced ethical dilemmas in combat situations, irrespective of whether they were military or civilian.[42]

The researchers also found that training effectiveness is likely best tested under conditions similar to those in operations that will stress the training audiences. Further, they found that timing is important, and that immediate superiors need to reinforce norms of restraint at critical times during soldiers' operational experiences, such as after a unit has experienced casualties in combat. Lastly, they concluded that norms of restraint are more likely to be followed if soldiers internalize them as part of their identity as soldiers.[43]

One final finding in "The Roots of Restraint in War" study is particularly important in terms of identifying ways to make IHL training more effective and the degree of effectiveness more measurable. The researchers pointed out that "youth make up the bulk of present and future fighters. Finding innovative and locally adapted ways to reinforce norms of humanity among them, including via digital media, is essential."[44] Today, the popularity of war video games is increasing every year, particularly the so-called first-person shooter games,[45] but there is serious debate in academia[46] and in the war video game industry itself[47] as to the propriety and effects of representations of armed conflict and what this means for the game players.

The use of war video games as educational and training tools will be discussed in more detail in the review of different cases studies in Chapter 5. Because these games are likely to increase in significance over time, it is worthwhile here to briefly note some of the complexities of using them and the unsettled nature of the research surrounding their use. Recent research suggests that many who play video games experience positive mental health benefits from gaming,[48] and that even video games with content that is largely about armed conflict can have therapeutic effects on veterans suffering from mental health issues such as posttraumatic stress disorder (PTSD).[49]

Conversely, other research suggests that players of violent video games can become desensitized to real-life violence and lose empathy regarding others' suffering.[50] Some anecdotal reports indicate that for soldiers who play war video games, their virtual experiences prepare them poorly for their psychological reactions when they actually take human life.[51] In addition, although their work is deadly serious, the remote pilots who fly drones on combat missions from thousands of miles away perhaps perceive their operational environment in a manner similar to that of a computer simulation or a war video game. From an emotional perspective, though, they can experience very high levels of stress because of the nature of their work.[52] All of this suggests that significant research on video gaming as a means of providing effective IHL instruction is likely required before militaries begin making full-scale use of it for this purpose.

Analysis

Just as the ICRC followed up on "The Roots of Behaviour in War" study with "The Roots of Restraint in War" report in 2018, it reassessed the ground covered by the 1999 "People on War" survey in a similar 2016 survey. Importantly, this survey interviewed people from the same nations that were part of the earlier project. The results of the 2016 survey provide a sobering backdrop against which to assess the significance of these two studies in terms of the effectiveness of IHL education and training efforts in general across the world.

In total, 17,762 people were interviewed, using a battery of 20 main questions, some of which closely tracked questions that were asked in the original survey.[53] The responses to three of the questions are particularly pertinent to efforts to increase the effectiveness of IHL training: what the respondents believed the effect of IHL on armed conflict to be, what they believed were the most important ways to reduce the number of victims of war, and whom they believed had the most influence in determining whether troops follow IHL. The results of this survey show without any doubt that improving the effectiveness of IHL training must be an urgent priority for the international community and national militaries.

Regarding the effectiveness of IHL, 37 percent of the respondents from the states affected by conflict believed that IHL made no real difference in how armed conflict played out, whereas 42 percent of the respondents from the UN Security Council permanent members plus Switzerland believed this to be so, for a total of 41 percent. This is troubling because in 1999 a total of only 36 percent held this opinion, and this is a statistically significant decrease in respondents' assessment of IHL efficacy. Further, while a total of 52 percent of respondents believed that IHL kept wars from becoming worse in the 1999 "People on War" study, only 38 percent believed this in 2016—again, a statistically significant drop.[54] Consistent with these results, the number of Swiss and UN Security Council permanent member respondents who believed that increasing the effectiveness of IHL was an important, or somewhat important, option to reduce casualties dropped from 80 percent in 1999 to 71 percent in 2016, another statistically significant decline.[55]

A total of 81 percent of respondents saw military leaders as having the most significant role in keeping troops compliant with IHL, more so by those living in countries affected by armed combat (84 percent) than those living in Switzerland or the UN Security Council permanent members (80 percent). The next most influential group identified by the respondents were combatants' peers, at 67 percent.[56] Viewed against the significant decrease in international public confidence in the value of IHL, and the common sense recognition by the international public as to the identity of the people who are most likely to impact IHL compliance by soldiers, the findings of "The Roots of Restraint in War" study present a meaningful path forward in correcting this deficit. Emphasizing only the legal bases of IHL norms is simply not sufficient; there must also be an engagement with leaders and soldiers on the platform of values. These values must include collective military identities and senses of professionalism, and this engagement must be guided by data rather than traditional assumptions.

To place these results in context, it is also important to note that in a 2019 ICRC survey of 16,288 Millennial respondents (ages 20–35), 54 percent agreed with the statement that the Geneva Conventions helped reduce suffering in armed conflict. Respondents in only two neighboring countries, Syria and Israel (56 and 53 percent, respectively), were a majority in believing that the Geneva Conventions did not really make a difference in this regard.[57] These responses suggest that there may be marked differences in attitudes toward IHL depending upon a person's age group, and this could have implications for IHL education and training. In the end, however, receiving a positive response from slightly more than half of those surveyed is hardly a ringing endorsement of IHL's perceived value among any age group.

Summary

Now, rather than swimming against the tide of unit cohesion and the impacts of military authority, the ICRC recognizes that the positive aspects of efforts to build unit and professional identities could also be used to provide a meaningful ethical and emotional grounding for IHL compliance in the individual soldier. Also, soldiers possess agency in deciding when and how they will act on these values. While there may certainly be many commonalities, these values and the ways in which they are expressed, and the means by which they are internalized by individual soldiers, will likely vary from country to country, and perhaps even from unit to unit. Further, long-standing assumptions as to who are the most credible carriers of the IHL message in education and training need to be reassessed, and the results of these reassessments may likewise vary from country to country. There is no single universal answer, but the role of leaders and comrades clearly must be part of a more effective approach to making IHL training more effective.

Data does not support the idea that instruction on IHL, coupled with sanctions for violations of it, is the main driver of compliance with IHL. The data confirms that soldiers are human, and that their fellow members of the international community recognize the role that soldiers' leaders and comrades play in whether they will comply with IHL. Across the world, people are very concerned that the IHL these soldiers apply in their operations is no longer as effective as it once was in protecting those not in combat. Traditional methods of IHL instruction that focus on the content of the law and ignore the values context in which it is understood, and that do not take account of the role of leaders in developing these understandings through informal socialization as well as formal military authority, are unlikely to reverse this trend.

Crucially, working with these understandings must be based on assessment, which must be driven by the collection of objective and meaningful data. There is always the risk that programs of data collection might lose their focus, and that data collection becomes a goal itself rather than being timed for the harvesting of information that is of maximum value in a minimally disruptive way. With this in mind, it is now useful to again set the clock back 20 years and to turn to data from a group of officers who were probably the closest in understanding what their unit NCOs and soldiers were thinking and feeling about IHL instruction and training, while at the same time exercising full command authority over them—high-performing company-grade commanders who had recently been promoted to field-grade rank.

Chapter 2

COMMAND & GENERAL STAFF COLLEGE CLASS OF 2002

In late October 2001, the military law instructors at CGSC asked US student officers from selected services and service branches to participate in a survey regarding their experiences with IHL and IHL-related training.[1] The vast majority of those asked to take the survey were Army officers, but 22 were Marines. With only one exception, the officers had all been fairly recently promoted to major and therefore had about 10 years of commissioned service. This level of experience for these students remains constant today—98 percent of the officers in the Class of 2021, for example, were in the Year Group 2010 cohort, that is, they had been commissioned as second lieutenants in 2010.[2] The purpose of the survey was to begin the development of an empirical database on the efficacy of IHL training to use to improve instruction on IHL in the context of leadership development at CGSC. Unfortunately, that project never proceeded past the initial survey, and the data from it was never published. The results, however, are still relevant today to the question of IHL training effectiveness.

Survey Parameters

The survey students came predominately from the Command and General Staff Officer Course, but a number had already graduated from the course the year before and had been selected to attend the postgraduate School for Advanced Military Studies, one of the schools comprising CGSC.[3] The military law instructors selected Army officers in the Armor, Engineer, Field Artillery, Infantry, Military Intelligence, Military Police, and Special Forces branches. The instructors chose these branches based on a survey design assumption that soldiers from these branches were likely to have experienced operational deployments that had necessitated training in situations involving the use of up to, and including, lethal force.[4]

At that point in time, the officers who were selected to attend the resident course at Fort Leavenworth had been evaluated as being in the top half of their year group cohort.[5] Because the US Marine Corps' mission and its "deeply egalitarian, tradition-based culture" result in a high degree of uniformity in career paths and tactical experiences irrespective of individual officers' military occupational specialties,[6] all of the Marine students at the college were asked to be survey participants, although half were in combat support and combat service support branches.[7]

In keeping with the CGSC policy, the survey was anonymous and voluntary and was delivered in hard copy to students' individual mailboxes. The survey had two portions. The first portion contained 37 questions designed to elicit responses that could be easily quantified. These questions gathered demographic, experiential, and training assessment data and were retrospective.[8]

The second portion was qualitative and prospective and consisted of two questions: (1) "How would you improve LOW [law of war] and/or ROE training in general?" and (2) "What challenges do you see for future LOW and/or ROE training as our armed forces deal with transnational and subnational actors such as terrorist groups and criminal syndicates?" As to these questions, there were 146 responses to the question regarding how to improve IHL and IHL-related training, and there were 119 responses to the question about future challenges to effective training.[9]

Survey Respondent Demographics

Of the 401 officers requested to participate in the survey, 188 submitted responses. With one important exception, the percentages of Army officers who replied to the survey were either identical to or closely matched their branches' respective percentages in the survey group as a whole, rounded to the nearest whole integer. For example, 12 percent of the questionnaires were delivered to Armor officers, and 13 percent of the responses came from Armor officers. About half of the Marines who received copies of the survey responded. Despite the small number of Marines surveyed, their rate of response as a group was roughly equivalent to the Army officers' rate as a whole.

Had the survey been conducted with greater rigor, for example, if the recipients of the survey instrument had been chosen at random, the response rate would have suggested a 5 percent margin of error. Regardless, the fact that about half of the officers in each of the branches responded suggests that the results were fairly representative of the group as a whole.[10] The exception to this pattern of response was Special Forces. None of the 30 Army Special Forces officers responded.

Leadership experience

In terms of their leadership experience, the respondents were a seasoned group. Only 3 percent of the respondents had less than 13 months' time in company-grade command, that is, in command of a unit of approximately 200 troops.[11] Thirty percent had between 13 and 18 months, and 30 percent had between 19 and 24 months. Thirty-seven percent had over 25 months' time in command. An ordinary Army company-grade command would last at least 12 months and optimally 18 months.[12] The large number of officers with more than two years' time in command suggests that they were successful leaders at that level and may have had successive commands as captains. If this were the case, it might lend greater weight to their impressions and assessments of IHL and IHL-related training, because they ideally would have experienced more IHL training while in command. A more refined survey instrument would have sought to correlate time in command with the number of command positions held by the respondents.[13]

Training experience

The respondents were also quite familiar with the large-scale unit training exercises conducted at the Army or Marine Corps combat training centers, such as the Army's Joint Readiness Training Center at Fort Polk, Louisiana.[14] Only 2 percent had never experienced a training center rotation. Sixty percent had rotated through a training center between one and six times, which would appear to be consistent with the 18-month training center cycle most units appear to have followed during this time.[15] Twenty-eight percent had experienced more than seven training exercises at one of these centers, and 19 percent had experienced 10 or more rotations. This might be because 26 percent of the respondents had served as training observers/controllers at these centers at some point in their careers. It is not possible to confirm this; it was a flaw in the survey design to not ask respondents to disaggregate their experiences at the training centers as training participants rather than as training cadre.[16]

Operational experience

In terms of their operational experiences, the survey respondents were also a seasoned group. Only 8 percent had not deployed. Seventy-eight percent had deployed operationally between one and three times, but only 14 percent had deployed more than three times. As to the types of deployments, the respondents could choose multiple types, and the largest single category

(45 percent) was combat. This was followed by peace enforcement deployments (40 percent), operational training deployments (26 percent), humanitarian operations (24 percent), peacekeeping (13 percent), and finally noncombatant evacuation operations (1 percent).[17]

Frequency and Length of IHL and IHL-Related Training

Although the survey sought to capture experiences and impressions gathered over the course of these officers' careers, it was intended to focus on those times when the officers would have been in company-grade command. The responses to the question as to when IHL and IHL-related training was received in their last assignment with soldiers and Marines provided some interesting answers. On the healthy side, 26 percent stated that it had occurred more than once a year, 31 percent stated that it had occurred annually, and 40 percent stated that it had occurred in predeployment training. On the other hand, 3 percent stated that it had not occurred. A more refined survey instrument would have asked those who stated "never" why it had not been accomplished—this might provide useful information for even contemporary trainers to better understand where there might be gaps in unit training plans in terms of IHL training execution.[18]

Interestingly, the amount of time allotted for this training varied widely among the respondents. Fifty-seven percent had at least half a day devoted to IHL and IHL-related training. Twenty-four percent of the respondents' units had trained on these topics for between two and four days, and 7 percent for at least one work week. Surprisingly, 9 percent were able to devote more than a week to this training. This suggests another possible error in the survey. Respondents might have confused the length of IHL training with the length of training exercises as a whole that had IHL events embedded in them. Had the survey been in greater depth, it would have been useful to explore the specific topic areas and the methods of delivery that were used for the multiday training by these former commanders.[19]

Delivery of IHL and IHL-Related Training

The respondents were asked what different methods of IHL and IHL-related training had been used in their last assignments with troops. This question allowed them to provide multiple answers as appropriate. Not surprisingly, 82 percent had received this training through a PowerPoint presentation. Next in frequency, with a response rate of 76 percent, were verbal briefings; discussions and seminars at 56 percent; situational training exercises in specific training lanes using role players (so-called STX lanes) at 37 percent; video clips at 36 percent; after action reviews following field exercises or combat training center rotations at 21 percent; and within field training exercises themselves at 15 percent.[20]

When asked to correlate the efficacy of these different training delivery methods with different training audiences, the respondents provided some interesting assessments. For officers and senior NCO training, the respondents' efficacy assessments for field training exercise or training center rotation after action reports, field training exercises, video clips, and verbal briefings all registered between 20 and 24 percent—not particularly high. PowerPoint briefings were rated marginally higher at 28 percent. Whether they found STX lane training to be effective for officers and senior NCOs, however, was an even split at 50 percent. By far, the respondents evaluated discussions and seminars as the most effective training delivery method for officers and senior NCOs, at 78 percent—although, as noted above, only 56 percent said they had used this method. A more in-depth survey would have explored this apparent disconnect to determine why this method was not used more often if it were so effective.[21]

The cause of this inconsistency might have been the unavailability of discussion- or seminar-format lesson plans for officers and senior NCOs that were designed for use at the company or battery level. Perhaps those that did exist required a greater investment in preparation and delivery time than the small unit commanders could afford on their training schedules. Perhaps there were not enough qualified and competent instructors available to make these sorts of lesson plans work at the small unit level. If this last possibility were the case, one might assume that legal advisors would be a useful resource to remedy this deficit, yet half of the respondents stated that legal advisors were rarely, if ever, necessary in planning IHL or IHL-related training in their units.[22]

When it came to training efficacy with junior enlisted troops, 70 percent of the respondents found STX lanes to be effective. The next most effective delivery method was the discussion or seminar format, at 49 percent. The least effective types of training delivery were after action reports from field training exercises or training center rotations and PowerPoint briefings, both at 16 percent. Verbal briefings were seen as being marginally more effective, at 20 percent, as were field training exercises at 22 percent. Video clips were seen as being more effective for junior enlisted (35 percent) than they were for officers and senior NCOs (24 percent). These figures suggest that an IHL training program that used STX lanes in conjunction with discussion- or seminar-format instruction utilizing video clips could have been particularly useful for the respondents' junior troops.[23]

The Relationships of IHL and IHL-Related Training to Mission Objectives, Training Objectives, and Performance Deficiencies

In response to the question as to how frequently their units received IHL or IHL-related training that was tailored to their missions, 37 percent of the respondents found that this happened infrequently or never. Similarly, 42 percent found that this training was infrequently or never tailored to their units' training objectives. More tellingly, 63 percent found that the training they received was infrequently or never tailored to training deficiencies identified in their units. A more refined survey would have asked how these training deficiencies were identified and prioritized, or whether such efforts had even occurred.[24]

These results raise some important questions. Taken in context, they suggest that a great deal of IHL training done at the small unit level while the respondents were in command was delivered using a standard format, potentially the dreaded slide deck presentation, with a low level of interaction between the instructors and the training audiences. On the one hand, there is certainly value in ensuring that all troops in a larger formation, such as a battalion or higher, are trained to the same standard, and the use of an officially vetted and approved presentation might seem like an efficient way to accomplish this.

Conversely though, to make sure that company-sized unit training in these important areas is effective, training delivery and content should be keyed to remediating gaps in IHL understanding at this level. A survey conducted in greater depth would have sought to determine how many of the 50 percent of respondents who found it unnecessary to work with their legal advisors to conduct this training were among those who also believed their units' training needs were not being met in important ways.[25] Digging even deeper, a better survey would also have asked respondents to identify the methodologies they used to identify IHL training gaps.

The Value of Role Players in Situational Training Exercises

The respondents' assessment of the use of role players in STX lanes to replicate civilians who might be found on the battlefield stood out as very positive. Sixty percent stated that in their home station training prior to operational deployments, they often experienced the use of role players. Twenty-two percent found this training to be realistic and challenging, and 45 percent found it useful, although imperfect. Only 3 percent found it to be unrealistic. Three-quarters of the respondents had experienced role players during their training center rotations, and 43 percent assessed them as providing realistic and challenging training, and the same number assessed this training to be useful if imperfect. Only 1 percent found this training to be unrealistic.[26] The differences in the assessments of home station versus training center role play training regarding role player realism could be due to several factors. For example, role players at units' home stations might have been organized on an ad hoc basis,[27] while those at the combat training centers continuously learned to hone their role-playing skills and, therefore, more deeply developed their range of actions and reactions in their scenarios.[28]

The combat training center role players did receive high marks for the quality of their contributions. Ninety-two percent of the respondents who had been through rotations and experienced role play scenarios found the role players had acted realistically, and 97 percent believed that the role players understood their roles. Importantly, 88 percent found the role players were flexible and able to adapt to scenario free play as the action in the STX lanes developed, and 81 percent found the role players had properly stayed true to their roles. Importantly, 87 percent found that the role players had provided meaningful feedback to their troops upon the completion of the scenarios.[29] It is difficult to overstate the value of immediate feedback, unvarnished by staffing processes and higher unit agendas, to the soldiers while they were training, from sources their commanders agreed were quite credible. Potentially then, role players are also an important target audience for IHL training.

The Purpose of Complying with IHL

From a legal perspective, whether enemy combatants act in conformance with IHL is not relevant to the question of whether one's own soldiers must follow it. Reciprocity is not a precondition for complying with IHL.[30] From a practical perspective, however, encouraging reciprocity in IHL compliance has often been used as a practical example as to why troops should comply with IHL.[31] The survey sought to explore this distinction by asking the respondents to address whether the training they had experienced had adequately explained why troops are expected to follow IHL, and whether they thought enemy soldiers' compliance with IHL was an important factor in whether US troops would comply with IHL themselves.

As to the first question, 86 percent agreed that IHL training had in their experience adequately addressed the rationale behind IHL compliance. A more refined survey would have asked the respondents what they believed the rationales behind IHL compliance to be, other than just that it was the law. Regardless, to put this figure in context, 85 percent agreed that IHL compliance by adversaries was an important fact in US troops continuing to comply.[32] It is clear these former commanders believed that their troops might very well key their compliance to actual reciprocity. This suggests that the young majors recognized that this was a realistic problem, and that a different tangible reason for compliance needed to be made part of training.

Improving IHL and IHL-Related Training

One hundred and forty-six respondents expanded upon their quantitative answers when asked to suggest ways in which IHL and IHL-related training could be improved. Thirty-seven of these responses dealt with the need to standardize and integrate this training. These respondents believed that this should occur across the timeline of military service, from basic training all the way through the different levels of service schools, and in training center rotations as well. The respondents were clear that this training should not be conducted via briefings as "additional training." One respondent noted that instructors needed to avoid the usual "LOW and ROE training events (i.e., briefings or PowerPoint presentations). Rather, it should be an additional training objective for unit training and leveraged on existing training so soldiers practice it throughout the year." The respondents also believed that giving troops practical experience with legal issues woven into tactical scenarios throughout the spectrum of training events would be most effective, particularly when tailored to the experiences of the audience.[33]

Nineteen responses addressed the scenarios that had been used in training they experienced. The respondents noted significant concerns with the realism and rigor of a number of the scenarios. One respondent noted that for scenario-driven training to be most effective, it needed to present troops with the full range of possible threats that could occur. Stated one, "The scenarios never get to the point where shots in self-defense are fired. We need to work through the entire scale of escalation."

Other respondents noted that sometimes units would take actions in training that let them avoid having to deal with role players portraying civilians on the battlefield, and one noted that the scenarios "should emphasize the higher priority" of interaction with these role players. One respondent noted that scenarios should include more irregular combatants and civilians mixed in with "captured personnel to ensure that soldiers know how to treat captured and detained personnel." Finally, two respondents suggested going beyond strict IHL and ROE issues in the scenarios and placing troops in difficult ethical dilemmas as well.[34]

Challenges in Future IHL and IHL-Related Training

Nature of the conflict

One hundred and nineteen respondents expanded upon their quantitative answers when asked to identify what the future challenges for effective IHL training would be. It is important to note that their responses might have been significantly impacted by the six weeks between the Al Qaeda attacks and the distribution of the survey at the end of October 2001. In fact, 20 respondents, the second-largest number of respondents to this question, identified adversaries' noncompliance with IHL as a training challenge, and 11 referenced these attacks directly or indirectly in their responses.

One typical response was that the "war on terrorism and 9/11 events will make it difficult to get young soldiers to buy into the validity of [IHL]. It will be tough for us as a force." Importantly, eight of these respondents believed that this was a challenge that could be overcome, with steps such as increased command emphasis on IHL training, appealing to troops' sense of honor as military professionals, and by explaining the practical negative impacts of US forces failing to comply with expected standards.[35]

Training scenario relevance

The largest group of respondents, 23, were concerned about the effectiveness of scenarios that were used in training. Only five respondents directly or indirectly expressed concern about the efficacy of existing scenario-based training to deal effectively with troops encountering irregular combatants on the battlefield. One of these respondents stated, "Training exercises are too short to adequately portray the patience, cunning, and deliberations that terrorists possess. Often times, training exercises are spoiled by throwing in every worst case scenario in a 24-hour period, i.e., carjackings, logistics bombings, and too [many] suicide bombers."[36] This is just one response, but it is in marked contrast to the point noted by one respondent earlier that scenarios used in training did not illustrate the full range of threats that soldiers might face in operations. Taken together, perhaps these two points call for the number of scenario threats to be calibrated with the intensity of the risks posed by those threats to make the scenarios most relevant.

Training scenario realism

The largest number of these respondents, 13, were concerned about the realism of the scenarios used in training. Features of realistic training suggested by these respondents included greater use of role players, the inclusion of language and cultural aspects of the expected theaters of operation into the scenarios, and expanding the breadth of scenario training. One respondent acknowledged the importance of showing "soldiers what they'll experience on operational deployments." He then noted an important limitation that commanders would need to be mindful of—"We don't absolutely know their reactions (ethical decision making) until some of their buddies get hurt or killed. This is the true test of restraint as a result of ethical decision making." This respondent noted that this type of situation could not be replicated in a standard simulated combat training event. Thus, "there may be no solution to the problem unless trainers can induce a like stress as is done at Ranger School through food and sleep" deprivation.[37]

Distinguishing those not in combat and the role of ROE

The last major category of responses, from 17 respondents, dealt with the challenges of training troops to properly distinguish between civilians and combatants in operations. These respondents were concerned with the difficulties of dealing with crowds of civilians, in general, and the difficulties inherent in separating out combatants from these groups, in particular. They were concerned that the criteria for making these distinctions were vague and unhelpful to troops in stressful situations. In a singular view that foreshadowed IHL detention issues, one respondent suggested that "role-playing captured Al Qaeda members will be helpful during the war on terrorism."[38]

Although 14 respondents recognized that there could be potential problems with different sets of ROE depending on the operation, both national and multinational, and that this would need to be addressed in training, only three respondents had the impression that troops did not recognize the importance of ROE, and only two thought that IHL and ROE training were not sufficiently integrated. Only one respondent thought that there were insufficient numbers of military attorneys available to assist in training. In contrast to these impressions, only five respondents thought there was too much emphasis on IHL and ROE in training.[39] A more refined survey might seek to correlate these findings with the length of IHL training the respondents had received at their units.

Special Forces

The reason for the zero response rate by the Special Forces officers was never identified, because querying them in person would not have been in keeping with the anonymous and voluntary nature of the survey. Well-known instances of IHL violations by special forces troops in the US military, such as those charged in the court-martial of the US Navy SEAL Chief Gallagher,[40] and in the Australian special forces as documented in the Brereton Report, have drawn attention to these communities. They have also emphasized the role of leadership ethics in these units and the insularity that characterizes their operations and culture. This suggests that the decision by the Class of 2002 Special Forces officers to not participate in the survey should not be viewed as a survey error, but instead as a data point itself in considering how to make IHL education and training more effective for these units.

A US Marine Corps publication on case studies of operational culture provides a useful perspective on the nature of US special forces' organizational culture. In this book, Aragon, a senior officer who had originally been a regular US Air Force pilot, related his transition from flying bombers to flying special operations tactical intelligence, surveillance, and reconnaissance aircraft. His overall assessment of his new operational community was forthright and concise: "The culture of Special Operations Forces (SOF) consists of behavior and characteristics that would make any conventionally trained airman fearful of a court-martial."[41]

Helpfully though, Aragon went further and identified three factors that made special forces so different from regular forces. First, as to their social structure, rank was only "loosely coupled with authority, while experience within the unit often defined who was in charge, at least informally." Second, unlike regular units, their political structure and chains of authority were not defined by an obvious hierarchy of control. Instead, the command lines were blurry, and "chain of command and approval authorities often resided with whomever our 'customer' was on a particular day." Finally, their core operational values were different. To Aragon, "the SOF belief system was founded on a history of innovators and mavericks who challenged the established order" and had rejected conventional operational paradigms as they fashioned their own solutions to complex problems.[42]

It is certainly not the case that US Army Special Forces are disinterested in training IHL, and they have also used it to increase small unit effectiveness among the troops from other nations with whom they work.[43] The zero response rate to the survey suggests, though, that attempts to survey this particular military community might need to be specifically tailored and delivered in ways different from those found adequate for their regular Army colleagues.[44] This also suggests that the remedial training measures recommended in the Brereton Report, such as educating Australian special forces troops on the causes of war crimes by their colleagues,[45] would need to be carefully constructed and delivered to be seen as credible by these troops. As Mastroanni has realistically noted, "Service members are well aware that there are sometimes those among them who fail to uphold those standards"[46]—troops in these tightly knit units will likely know much better than any outside instructor what the causes of these war crimes were.

Analysis

This survey had limitations, and if the database development project had been carried forward, it would have been necessary to rework certain areas of questions to develop more complete and accurate data. However, the results raise several points regarding IHL training that the students had experienced that warrant further consideration, especially training involving role players, the use of seminar- or discussion-format IHL training for both leaders and junior troops, the motivation for following IHL when enemies do not, and the fact that the respondents generally did not forecast the impact of insurgent warfare upon IHL training for their troops.

STX lanes and role players

Regarding role play, the greatest number of respondents (70 percent) assessed that experiential training in the form of STX lanes with role players was an effective IHL training method for junior enlisted. Their own assessments of the usefulness of this training were likewise positive. Sixty-seven percent found such training done at home station prior to deployment to be at least useful, and this increased to 86 percent for this sort of training during the combat training center rotations. Consistent with this, the role players at the training centers received very high evaluations for the realism and quality of their exercise play.[47] These results suggest that on the eve of the US deployment into Afghanistan, the former company-grade commanders had already concluded that role playing was a very useful training tool in this regard.

Although role play and role players in particular received high marks for effectiveness, the largest group of answers to the question regarding future challenges in training IHL focused on the effectiveness of the scenarios used in the training lanes themselves (23 respondents). Of these 13 respondents specifically questioned the realism of the scenarios and whether they actually portrayed what the troops might encounter. Similarly, in response to the question as to how they would improve IHL training, 19 respondents expressed negative views regarding the realism and rigor of the scenarios they had experienced.[48]

Such concerns unfortunately manifested themselves at Abu Ghraib prison, for example, where the investigating officer, US Army Major General Taguba, found "very little instruction or training was provided to [Military Police] personnel on the applicable rules of the Geneva Convention Relative to the Treatment of Prisoners of War."[49] Taken all together, these points suggest an assessment of STX lanes and role players by the survey respondents not dissimilar from what one might read in a movie review—the acting was great, but the plot, not so much. Contemporary surveys could benefit by exploring whether such a perception exists among new field-grade officers today.

Seminar- or discussion-format IHL training

Interestingly, although the respondents identified STX lane training to be the most effective of the different types of training for junior enlisted troops, half of them also believed that discussion- or seminar-style IHL training for these young soldiers would also be an effective way to train them. Slightly more than half had used this method apparently, although it is not possible from the survey results to determine whether they had experienced this form of training with junior enlisted or just fellow officers and NCOs. Regardless, this suggests that there was a recognized need for this type of instruction.

One might assume that military attorneys would have been a logical resource for these former commanders to use to help meet this demand. As noted earlier, however, half of the respondents believed working with their legal advisors was largely unnecessary to conduct IHL training.[50] Only one respondent believed that there were insufficient numbers of military attorneys to assist in the training.

A more thorough survey might have asked whether respondents who had experienced the use of discussion- or seminar-style IHL instruction were also among those who found that their military attorneys were helpful in executing IHL training. Even if this were the case, though, just as a matter of numbers, it is doubtful that there would have been sufficient lawyers supporting a typical brigade to be able to deliver IHL training in this format to all the brigade's junior enlisted. As will be discussed in Chapter 4 regarding battlefield ethics training in Iraq, however, with careful curriculum development the scarcity of lawyers need not be a bottleneck in delivering this sort of training to junior troops.

Reciprocity in IHL compliance

The survey results also suggested that IHL trainers needed to find a better practical reason for complying with IHL than the expectation that it would encourage reciprocity by the enemy. Eighty-five percent of the respondents identified adversaries not complying with IHL to be a major factor in their troops' decisions whether to comply themselves. In the qualitative portion of the survey, the second largest group of responses to the question as to challenges they foresaw to effective future IHL training (20 respondents) focused on this problem as well.[51] As will be discussed in Chapter 4, the eventual approach to this problem for the Army and the Marines was to try to take the traditional IHL principle of honor, or chivalry, and to rework it into a modern sense of honorable professionalism.

Distinction between combatants and civilians

Finally, although 17 respondents had identified distinguishing between combatants and civilians as a training challenge, it is interesting that only five of the respondents expressed concern about the efficacy of existing scenario-based training to allow troops to respond appropriately to irregular combatants they encountered on the battlefield. Likewise, of the 146 respondents who answered the question as to what they would improve in IHL training, only one stated that it was necessary to include more scenarios involving noncombatants mixed with irregular combatants. In hindsight, these results are puzzling—it appears that most of the respondents did not foresee that their former troops and successor commanders would soon be fighting intense counterinsurgencies.[52]

Perhaps this was due to a flaw in the survey question itself. Respondents were asked what challenges they foresaw in IHL training geared to dealing with "transnational and sub-national actors such as terrorist groups and criminal syndicates"—the survey did not specifically mention "insurgents."[53] It is also possible that the conventional Army's lack of emphasis on counterinsurgency in its doctrine and training after the Vietnam War led to a conceptual blind spot on the parts of both the survey designers and the respondents.[54] Perhaps it was also because the US government's position on its aims in Afghanistan around the time the survey was administered suggested it had no intent on remaining there once it removed the Taliban government and achieved its military aims against Al Qaeda.[55]

As operations in Afghanistan quickly showed, however, it can be very difficult to discern combatants from those not participating in combat when the insurgents blend into the civilian population. From a utilitarian perspective, Magruder has pointed out that deploying forces might only be able to recognize someone as an adversary in advance of encountering them if local civilians actually identify that specific person as being an insurgent. Often, it is not obvious that people are combatants in these types of combat encounters until they open fire.[56]

This can lead deploying forces to rely more heavily on other more ambiguous behavioral indicators to determine whether someone is a combatant, for example, if they are performing what is considered a hostile act or signaling hostile intent through their actions under the applicable ROE.[57] There is an inherent tension between these more expansive authorizations to use force and the need in counterinsurgencies to otherwise minimize casualties among local populations and damage to private property—even below levels otherwise permissible under IHL.[58] This likely complicates IHL training curriculum design and the training of role players for the predeployment training for these sorts of missions.

Summary

Although the survey instrument was far from perfect, its results highlight two very important areas of IHL and IHL-related education and training that deserve much more attention: the means of instruction delivery and the audiences receiving the instruction. As to the means of instruction, the value of well-trained role players in STX lanes for soldiers was recognized 20 years ago, and it continues to be recognized today. It is not just that the use of role players makes training more realistic because persons not in combat will be in the battlespaces where soldiers operate—the use of role players makes the training more human and requires those being trained to exercise judgment and not just execute previously rehearsed drills. Judgment implies assessment, and assessment requires metrics and perspectives, which can include moral values.

Respondents also identified a means of instruction for enlisted soldiers that they saw as being effective, but which frankly does not appear to be often used with these troops: discussion- or seminar-style instruction. Some might object to using this form of instruction with junior soldiers on grounds of lack of resources, or that such an approach would encourage soldiers to think too much rather than react to their orders immediately, thereby endangering themselves and their comrades. As will be detailed in Chapter 4's examination of the battlefield ethics training program used in Iraq by US troops in 2007 and 2008, the data shows that these concerns can be effectively addressed.

In terms of the audiences receiving IHL instruction, it is important to assess the career paths and professional and personal development of officers and troops to determine when they might receive IHL education and training and have it register the greatest effect. Similarly, there will likely be times in their careers when it will be most useful to harvest data regarding their experiences and impressions regarding IHL instruction and application. For young officers, one of those times is likely the transition from company- to field-grade rank, as they move from being the officers with command authority closest to the troops they lead to becoming mature staff officers and potential battalion and brigade commanders.

The survey of the IHL and IHL-related experiences and impressions of new combat arms and combat support majors at CGSC does not appear to have been repeated since it was administered in late 2001. From the perspective of increasing the effectiveness of IHL training, however, the survey results are more than just historical artifacts. Even with its flaws, the survey identified important points about IHL training that are still relevant today, including the need to reassess the ways in which IHL training is delivered to determine whether they are in fact effective, and how different branches within the same military service might require different IHL instructional approaches. The survey results also suggest that the operational experiences and military education and training officers have already had will color their forecasts of future training needs and challenges. One more point stands out—soldiers need a more solid reason to follow IHL than it is the law, and if they follow it, their enemies might reciprocate.

Mindful of this, let us turn now to Chapter 3, which seeks to put these historical survey results into a useful context that will allow us to question them further. As newly minted field-grade officers, the survey respondents were likely no more than a couple of years removed from their tours in company-grade command. For them to be students at the resident course at CGSC, those tours had to have been successful—the battalion and brigade commanders rating them must have believed they had led their troops well, and that their units were successful. Therefore, the next step is to look at the physical and psychological combat experiences of these troops as they found themselves fighting intense counterinsurgencies in Afghanistan and Iraq, and to identify possible relationships between these experiences and complying with IHL.

Chapter 3

BATTLEFIELD IHL COMPLIANCE ASSESSMENT

Beginning with the deployment into Afghanistan of US and coalition units in October 2001, and continuing with the invasion of Iraq in March 2003,[1] many of the troops that the new majors in the CGSC Class of 2002 had formerly commanded were likely deployed into high-intensity combat operations. In Iraq, the quick collapse of resistance by the Iraqi regular armed forces was soon followed by the collapse of the Iraqi state. As public order dissolved, US and coalition forces found themselves dealing with a dangerous insurgency and eventually a civil war as different factions and ethnic groups battled for power.[2]

As the level of violence and the number of civilian and US casualties increased, by the end of 2006, the US military concluded that it risked strategic failure unless it revised its approach in Iraq.[3] The so-called surge of US troops into Iraq in 2007 and the new counterinsurgency strategy they implemented was successful in reversing the flow of the conflict and eventually enabling the establishment of a more stable Iraqi state. These efforts also resulted in extended tour lengths for troops and intense combat as the coalition forces fought to gain the upper hand.[4]

Aware of the stress that combat conditions placed on troops, beginning in Iraq in 2003[5] and continuing through 2012 in Afghanistan,[6] different high-level operational commanders and chiefs of combatant command service elements requested assessments of the mental health and well-being of deployed troops in combat units. These assessments used both anonymous surveys of troops and focus groups to gather more detailed information. Although all the surveys contain useful data relevant to the effectiveness of IHL training in preventing violations, the parallel surveys conducted in Afghanistan[7] and Iraq[8] in 2007 as part of the fifth Mental Health Advisory Team (MHAT V) assessments are the most pertinent.

The MHAT V Reports

The MHAT V Afghanistan survey respondents included 699 soldiers assigned to brigade combat teams (BCTs) and 190 soldiers assigned to Task Force (TF) Phoenix conducting the US Army training and mentoring mission with Afghan security forces.[9] Because of the different missions of these two groups, which led to the BCT soldiers being more likely to experience more intense combat, the advisory team disaggregated the results from the two different populations in certain areas.[10] This does not mean the work of the TF Phoenix soldiers was not stressful or dangerous, but because of the BCT soldiers' direct combat mission, their survey results are likely more useful to consider from the perspective of IHL training effectiveness, and these soldiers' mission was closer to that of their colleagues in Iraq.

There were two focus areas of the MHAT V survey analysis that are particularly important. First, the survey team was designed to assess "the mental health and well-being of the deployed force" and to identify trends by comparing the findings from Afghanistan with those from Iraq, and by comparing the findings from the MHAT V Afghanistan and Iraq surveys with earlier assessments that had been conducted in both countries.[11] As a result of this approach, the MHAT V Afghanistan report provides much more than just a snapshot of the mental health experiences of the units in Afghanistan at that time.

The second important focus area was one that stands out as being unique in the efforts to understand the significance of IHL and IHL-related training— the advisory team was also designed to assess "ethical issues faced by Soldiers to enhance future battlefield ethics training." The report notes that this aspect of MHAT V's mission had been "included in a previous MHAT (MHAT IV) at the specific request of the [commanding general], Multi National Forces-Iraq (MNF-I)."[12] It is not clear, however, that the Army Central Command service chief who requested the MHAT V survey in Afghanistan in 2007 specifically asked for this particular assessment.

The report does not indicate whether this survey team consulted with legal advisors on the phrasing of the questions probing ethical issues on the battlefield. The earlier MHAT IV report states that "other military subject matter experts" assisted the MHAT IV survey team in developing the ethical issue questions, but it does not list their areas of expertise.[13] Regardless, the questions have a direct bearing on IHL issues, and for the purposes of eliciting accurate information from soldiers regarding their attitudes and behaviors related to IHL and those of their unit members, they serve as decent proxies for questions specifically on legal issues. In this sense, the report's correlations of mental health factors to IHL compliance, and crucially even rates of compliance by the soldiers themselves and their comrades, provide an unprecedented opportunity to explore these factors together even as the survey respondents themselves were on the battlefield.

General Mental Health

As to their general levels of mental health, the MHAT V Afghanistan soldiers experienced statistically significant higher rates of depression compared to their colleagues in Iraq, 11 versus 6.9 percent. When the results were controlled for gender, rank, and time in theater, the combat soldiers in Afghanistan still experienced statistically higher rates of mental health issues in general, and depression and anxiety in particular. The unadjusted rates of experiencing acute stress were essentially identical, however, 15.3 percent for the soldiers in Afghanistan and 15.2 percent for those in Iraq.

Unfortunately, 15 percent of these soldiers in Afghanistan indicated a positive response for some level of suicidal ideation in the prior month, as did 13 percent of their colleagues in Iraq. The difference between the two populations was not statistically significant.[14] Further, focus group sessions conducted with some of the respondents as part of the survey suggested that the extension of the deployment tour length from 12 to 15 months had a negative impact on the soldiers' sense of mental well-being.[15]

The statistics regarding the troops' use of prohibited mood- or perception-altering substances are also worthwhile to consider. The BCT troops in Afghanistan in 2007 reported essentially the same rate of alcohol use as did their colleagues in Iraq, about 8 percent, but the use of alcohol in Afghanistan had declined significantly from what had been reported in 2005 (12 percent). The rate of illegal drug use in Afghanistan in 2007 (2.6 percent) was similar to that in 2005 (2.3 percent), but it was higher than the reported use among the 2007 soldiers in Iraq.[16] US soldiers have been convicted at courts-martial for grave IHL violations in Afghanistan and Iraq in which alcohol[17] or illegal drug[18] use was involved, but these instances are uncommon.

Unethical Behaviors

The section of the survey addressing so-called unethical behaviors deserves particular attention, because the "questions specifically addressed the issue of battlefield ethics and the adequacy of battlefield ethical training for preparing Soldiers to conduct combat operations" in these countries. Because these questions had not been included in the 2005 Afghanistan survey, the MHAT V Afghanistan report could only compare the survey results in this area with the results of its sister survey in Iraq, with some references to the first survey that had included these questions, the earlier one conducted in Iraq in 2006.[19]

The survey asked a total of 21 questions in this focus area, distributed almost evenly among four dimensions. Dimension 1 addressed "Attitudes Regarding the Treatment of Insurgents and Non-Combatants." Dimension 2 addressed "Battlefield Ethical Behaviors and Decisions." Dimension 3 addressed "Reporting Ethical Violations." Dimension 4 addressed "Battlefield Ethics Training."[20]

The survey report provided a sample question for each of the dimensions. For example, in Dimension 1, soldiers were asked how strongly they agreed or disagreed with the statement, "All non-combatants should be treated with dignity and respect." In Dimension 2, soldiers were asked how frequently they "insulted and/or cursed non-combatants in their presence." In Dimension 3, they were asked how strongly they agreed or disagreed with the statement, "I would report a unit member for the mistreatment of a non-combatant." Finally, in Dimension 4, their responses were scored on a "Yes" or "No" scale, and the sample statement provided was, "The training I received in the proper (ethical) treatment of non-combatants was adequate."[21]

Although the advisory team acknowledged that the "attitudes regarding the treatment of insurgents and non-combatants (Dimension 1) may be influenced by training and may also be a pre-cursor to behavior," it assessed on the basis of social psychological literature that "the direct link between attitudes and actual behavior is quite weak," and therefore it focused on the unethical behaviors reported for the Dimension 2 questions regarding civilians and their property. In addition to the question regarding negative verbal behavior, the respondents were also asked whether they had "damaged and/or destroyed private property when it was not necessary," "physically hit/kicked a non-combatant when it was not necessary," observed unit members "modifying" "the [ROE] in order to accomplish the mission," and, finally, whether they observed unit members "ignoring" the "[ROE] in order to accomplish the mission."[22]

Based on these questions, there were largely no significant statistical differences between the soldiers in Afghanistan and Iraq in 2007 regarding the treatment of those not in combat. Nearly 12 percent of the soldiers in Iraq reported damaging private property when it was not necessary at least once, versus 9.8 percent of the soldiers in Afghanistan. Five percent of the soldiers in Iraq reported physically striking a person not in combat when it was not necessary, versus 3.9 percent in Afghanistan. There was a significant statistical difference, however, in negative verbal behavior, with 29.6 percent of the soldiers in Iraq reporting this behavior, versus 36.6 percent in Afghanistan.[23] These tendencies appeared to grow stronger over time. For example, a later analysis of the MHAT V Iraq data showed that soldiers who were in theater longer reported higher rates of unethical behaviors and were less willing to report a comrade for mistreating civilians.[24]

The incidence rate of negative verbal behavior was neither a positive thing itself nor likely to foster the development of favorable perceptions and attitudes regarding US armed forces among the host nation populations. Although certain research suggests a link between such behavior and other more violent forms of behavior,[25] it is probably more useful to look closely at the incidence rates of more serious violations, such as unnecessarily damaging civilian property or physically striking civilians. Importantly, these surveys were conducted anonymously in the context of a mental health assessment, so the soldiers were probably more inclined to report these instances truthfully.

Further, the questions were couched in terms that excluded instances of necessity, so the responses should not have included times when the troops interacted with civilians in exigent combat circumstances. Taken together, these surveys suggest that in combat deployments involving contact with civilian populations, even troops that had been trained in IHL and their ROE might physically assault civilians at least once without operational justification between 4 and 5 percent of the time. For a military force seeking to avoid all instances of violations, this number is a reality to be reckoned with.

Unethical Behaviors and Mental Health

Like the results obtained in earlier MHAT reports, the MHAT V Afghanistan researchers also identified a strong correlation between instances of unethical behaviors and mental health issues (anxiety, depression, and acute stress) for the soldiers in Afghanistan in 2007. "Specifically, Soldiers who [reported] any mental health problem were more than twice as likely to report engaging in unethical behaviors as those who did not screen positive for a mental health problem." For example, 60.7 percent of those who reported having a mental health issue reported negative verbal behavior toward civilians, and 22.2 percent reported damaging civilian property unnecessarily.[26]

By way of contrast, of those soldiers who reported no mental health issues, only 2.5 percent stated that they had physically struck a civilian unnecessarily at least once. For those who reported a mental health issue, this rate increased to 11.1 percent.[27] This relationship particularly held true for soldiers reporting high anger levels. For those who reported low levels of anger, only 1.1 percent also reported physically striking civilians unnecessarily. For those experiencing high levels, this rate increased to 7.1 percent.[28]

These survey results suggest that steps that could be taken to reduce troops' mental health issues in general and especially anger levels could also have a positive impact on their compliance with IHL as a result of improving their mental well-being. They also suggest that viewing mental health data in an IHL training context could be a fruitful approach for instructors seeking to calibrate their IHL teaching to the training audience's actual needs.

Reporting Violators

The 1949 Geneva Conventions established a duty on the part of the treaties' signatories to identify and prosecute persons accused of committing grave breaches of the convention and to take the necessary steps to suppress violations of IHL other than grave breaches.[29] Grave breaches include willful killing, torture or inhumane treatment, and serious injury to the body or health of a protected person.[30] Additional Protocol I amplified this duty and required that its signatories require their military commanders to report breaches of the 1949 Geneva Conventions and the protocol to the appropriate authorities. The ICRC Commentary on Additional Protocol I indicates that the term "commander" is to be interpreted broadly to include even junior enlisted soldiers serving in a leadership role, and that "an implied duty of reporting violations extends to everyone in the military."[31]

As noted in the introduction, the United States has not signed Additional Protocol I. As a matter of policy, however, to "ensure that commanders can exercise their responsibilities to implement and enforce the law of war," the US armed services are required to create programs that allow credible reports of war crimes and other IHL violations to be made through the chain of command or other appropriate channels, such as the military police. All US military personnel, Department of Defense civilian employees, and contractors have a duty to report these incidents. If commanders find that allegations are "not supported by credible information, the allegation will nonetheless be forwarded through the chain of command to the appropriate Combatant Commander with this determination."[32]

Regarding reporting instances of unethical behavior committed by fellow unit members, the MHAT V Afghanistan report noted that from the perspective of small unit interpersonal dynamics, "soldiers' willingness to report unit members for unethical behaviors almost certainly runs counter to the strong sense of bonding that occurs among unit members during the deployment." Thus, the advisory team was not surprised to find "soldiers are reluctant to report the ethical violations of unit members and this reluctance is consistent across theaters." Focusing then on the soldiers in Afghanistan in 2007, the lowest percentage of troops that would report comrades for IHL violations was in the case of unnecessary destruction of private property, at 31.7 percent. The highest percentage who would report was in the case of a comrade "injuring or killing an innocent non-combatant"—initially reassuring, perhaps, but amazingly, only 43 percent agreed that they would do this.[33]

In the other cases—mistreatment of those not in combat, stealing from them, violating ROE, and not following general orders—only approximately one-third of the respondents agreed that they would report.[34] By regulation, the duty to report these behaviors is one of the 10 Soldier's Rules that US Army military attorneys rely on as a core tenet of their IHL instruction.[35] This reluctance is troubling, and even if it did occur in a historical US Army survey population, it is a factor that contemporary IHL trainers as well as commanders should consider as they seek ways to have soldiers internalize IHL principles as part of a collective professional military identity.

Adequacy of Training

The MHAT V surveys also asked the troops in Afghanistan and Iraq to report whether they had received training in the "proper (ethical) treatment of non-combatants" and whether they believed it was adequate. The advisory teams got at the question of training adequacy both directly and indirectly. Adequacy was evaluated directly by simply asking if it was adequate and indirectly "by asking if the Soldier had encountered situations that were ethically difficult despite the training." In contrast to their colleagues in Iraq, significantly fewer soldiers in Afghanistan in 2007 reported having received the training (71.5 versus 81.1 percent in Iraq).[36]

Perhaps there was a problem with the way the question was worded. Maybe some of the respondents were uncertain what training in "ethical" treatment was, because both the troops in Iraq (84.4 percent) and the troops in Afghanistan (74.2 percent) agreed that they had "received training that made it clear how [they] should behave towards non-combatants."[37] Irrespective of which percentages are more accurate, the results for the troops in both theaters are a bit surprising because the mandatory requirement for predeployment IHL training conducted by Army military attorneys or qualified military paralegals under *Army Regulation 350-1, Army Training and Leader Development* had already been in effect since 2006.[38]

For those troops that reported receiving the training, their answers to the direct question of adequacy appear very positive. For example, although only 71.5 percent of the soldiers in Afghanistan in 2007 recalled receiving training in the "proper (ethical) treatment of non-combatants," 69.6 percent of the respondents found it to have been adequate, or over 97 percent of those who recalled receiving it. The troops' answers to the final question in this dimension, though, suggests that there might have been a training gap in this regard. Twenty-eight percent of the troops surveyed in Iraq and 24.6 percent of those surveyed in Afghanistan agreed that they had encountered ethical situations in which they did not know how they should respond.[39] Were a contemporary military population to be similarly surveyed, it would be very useful to drill down into the types of ethical situations the troops had confronted to determine whether these were related to IHL.

Mental Health Risk Factors Possibly Related to IHL Compliance

Helpfully, the MHAT V reports identified both risk factors and protective factors related to mental health and well-being that military leaders and healthcare professionals should be aware of so that they can take measures to improve the lot of their troops. Probably the most significant risk factor was combat experience, both in terms of specific instances of combat and the intensity level of those instances. Based on the number of combat events the 2007 Afghanistan soldiers reported, the advisory team divided them into groups of low, medium, or high combat exposure and then correlated these groups with reported levels of acute stress (PTSD) and any mental health problem in general.[40]

Among those with low levels of combat experience, only 4.3 percent reported symptoms of acute stress. Among soldiers who had experienced high levels of combat, this rate climbed to 26.9 percent. Similarly, soldiers who had experienced low levels of combat reported general mental health issues at a rate of 7 percent, but this increased to 33.3 percent for those who had experienced high levels. The MHAT V Afghanistan advisory team also noted a reported higher level of combat intensity in 2007 as compared to the 2005 Afghanistan survey, which they attributed to a change from more static operations in 2005 to more active counterinsurgency operations in 2007.[41]

Additional risk factors identified by the MHAT V Afghanistan advisory team were the lengths of deployments, the effects of multiple deployments, and sleep deprivation. Deployment length was identified by 61.3 percent of the soldiers in Afghanistan as a major concern, and this may have been associated with concerns regarding separation from their families, which registered as a main concern for 41.8 percent.[42] Interestingly, the MHAT V Iraq report suggested that although time in theater was "strongly predictive" of mental health problems among junior enlisted, it appeared that this was related more closely to the combat experiences of the troops during that time than the time itself.[43]

For these survey respondents who were on 15-month tours, mental health problem levels peaked in the tenth month and decreased in the months just prior to redeployment. Interestingly, this was irrespective of their further combat experiences.[44] These results suggest that any refresher IHL training that occurs during a combat deployment might be most useful just prior to or during the time of greatest mental health problem risk.

One of the most troubling findings was the degree to which multiple deployments were impacting the NCO corps. The MHAT V Afghanistan team noted that "in the first-time deployer group, 72% were junior enlisted, 21% were NCOs, and 7% percent officers." For those who had deployed multiple times, however, only 26 percent were junior enlisted, and the rate for officers only increased to 9 percent. For NCOs, however, this rate jumped to 65 percent.[45]

Although not broken out specifically in the MHAT V Afghanistan report, that study found that NCOs "who had deployed more than one time were at increased risk for a mental health problem compared to those who were on their first deployment."[46] The Joint-Military Health Advisory Team (J-MHAT) 7 survey conducted in 2010 on NCOs in Afghanistan found that those who were on their first deployment for at least nine months at the time of the survey experienced psychological problems at the rate of 14.3 percent. But for those on their third deployment, this rate climbed to 32.5 percent. Similarly, only 4.5 percent of first-tour NCO officers reported taking mental health medications, as compared to 15.2 percent of those who were on their third tour.[47]

As in many militaries, NCOs are the backbone of US ground forces, and they are the leaders with whom junior enlisted are most likely to be in direct contact throughout their deployments.[48] The 2018 "Roots of Restraint in War" study on IHL training effectiveness demonstrated the high degree to which junior enlisted Australian troops, for example, valued the opinions of their NCOs. If junior troops are expected to emulate the examples set by their NCOs in battlefield ethics, these findings suggest that to maximize IHL compliance at the troop level, militaries need to be more cognizant of the additional burdens being placed on the NCO corps from a mental health perspective.

This is not to suggest that NCOs with mental health issues pose a threat to IHL compliance themselves—there is no empirical evidence of this. Further, given the stigma still associated with seeking mental health care in an operational environment,[49] if such a notion gained traction among military personnel, it would only add to the burden these soldier-leaders already shoulder. What this does suggest, though, is that NCOs who have been deployed multiple times are perhaps at risk of not presenting the most effective examples of IHL-compliant attitudes to their troops if they are overburdened and not feeling well.

The lack of sleep is another mental health risk factor. Of the MHAT V Afghanistan respondents, 33.6 percent reported not getting enough sleep as a major concern. Approximately 17 percent reported taking mental health medications, and of these, half were using sleep medications.[50] Six percent of the respondents reported that they had been involved in accidents or had made mistakes during their deployment because of sleepiness. Meanwhile, their colleagues in Iraq reported they needed about six and a half hours of sleep to feel well rested, but on average only received about five and a half hours of sleep per night. The report noted that these figures fell short of the seven to eight hours of sleep a night "shown to be necessary to maintain optimal cognitive function."[51]

To put these numbers in context, though, 52.1 percent reported some degree of sleep deprivation, which could suggest that those who experienced sleep problems were receiving even less than the average amount of time sleeping that was reported. For example, of the junior enlisted troops who had been in theater for at least nine months but reported no sleep deprivation, only 11.7 percent were positive for depression, anxiety, or acute stress. Conversely, those troops in theater that length of time who reported two hours of sleep deprivation per night experienced these mental health issues at the rate of 23.1 percent.[52]

Mental Health Protective Factors

The MHAT V reports also assessed features in troops' lives and work that served a protective function. For example, the MHAT V Afghanistan report found that "soldiers who rate their leadership, both NCO and officer, highly are less likely to have mental health problems" irrespective of the level of combat they experienced.[53] This finding is consistent with research in the civilian workplace that has documented a similar relationship,[54] and the beneficial impact of the trust that develops among employees in their leaders when the "leaders' intentions are perceived [...] to be positive, and their intentions and behaviours to be honest."[55] Specifically for soldiers who reported mental health problems and who had experienced high levels of combat, 35 percent assessed the leadership of their NCOs as low. Conversely, for those who reported both a high level of combat experience and a high level of NCO leadership, only 18 percent reported mental health issues.[56]

The same relationship held true with officer leadership, with very similar percentages. Thirty-two percent of the soldiers with high levels of combat experience and low officer leadership reported mental health issues, while only 20 percent of those who experienced high officer leadership did.[57]

Interestingly, researchers found in a 2016 study of Royal Norwegian Navy cadets that good leadership also helps buffer performance deficiencies in subordinates associated with lack of sleep.[58] These findings emphasize the very real and pervasive impacts of good leadership and indirectly highlight the need to consider both company-grade officers and junior NCOs as special target audiences for tailored and more extensive IHL education and training.

To round out the statistical information provided by the survey results, the MHAT V advisory teams also conducted some troop focus groups. In these groups, the troops were asked about ethical situations they had encountered during their deployment. Many troops reported difficulty distinguishing combatants from civilians. As to the training they had received, many commented that it was "basically 'death by PowerPoint.'" The MHAT V Afghanistan report found that for many soldiers, "the training was often deemed inadequate or a waste of time."[59] Similar comments were gathered in the Iraq troop focus groups in 2007, with many voicing skepticism about the effectiveness of the training they received.[60] It is important to note that the focus group results regarding training adequacy were not necessarily as positive as the survey results regarding training adequacy. This highlights the importance in any assessment of IHL training effectiveness to not solely rely on any one form of evaluation but to use different assessment methods as crosschecks on each other.

Analysis

The 2007 MHAT V reports for Afghanistan and Iraq identified three categories of significant factors that weigh on the ability of leaders to keep their units compliant with IHL and soldiers to discipline themselves. The first category of factors is the presumably honest reporting by troops as to their behaviors that were not in compliance with IHL and their attitudes toward compliance, gathered in what might have been seen by them primarily as a medical assessment rather than one geared toward potential discipline. Whether the troops would have been so forthright in a survey done outside of a medical context is unknown. The second category consists of those factors that posed mental health risks to the soldiers, or which might have been actual negative mental health outcomes themselves, and which correlated with noncompliant troop behaviors. In the third category are those things which appeared to be protective of troops' mental health, and which could be possibly developed to be part of a more holistic and effective IHL training program.

Accuracy of the data

As to the first category, although the respondents to the anonymous surveys were presumably honest regarding their own noncompliant actions and those they observed of others, as well as their reluctance to report comrades who violated IHL, there is a large gap in the survey results between the actual occurrence of violations and the hypothetical reporting of them. For example, although only roughly one-third of respondents stated they would report a unit member for violations less significant than injuring or killing a person not in combat, only between 4 and 5 percent had actually physically struck a civilian when it was unnecessary. This suggests that the troops' individual levels of self-discipline were a more reliable indicator of unit compliance than was their likelihood to report violators among their comrades. If so, IHL education and training that resonated with their sense of ethical and professional self, or which recast the ethical dilemma of reporting a comrade as no longer being one of competing positive values—following the law versus personal loyalty— might register more favorably.

These questions in the 2006 and 2007 MHAT surveys appear to have been "the first systematic assessment of battlefield ethics in a combat environment since World War II."[61] The US military conducted extensive surveys of its military personnel in World War II, and it made use of the results to help guide decision-making about personnel policies and the development of units and equipment.[62] Some of these surveys also asked some very stark questions about attitudes related to IHL compliance.

For example, a survey conducted on 1,033 US airborne soldiers in Europe in May 1944 asked what the respondents would like to see happen to the Germans and the Japanese after the war. As to the German people, the largest group of respondents, 56 percent, chose the option "Punish the leaders but not the ordinary German." Regarding the Japanese people, however, the largest group of respondents, 72 percent, chose the option "Wipe out the whole Japanese nation."[63] It is shocking today to realize that genocide could be recognized as an acceptable suggested answer on an official survey, but it is a cautionary reminder of the power of gathering accurate data on frank and uncomfortable questions in a wartime environment.

Risk factors

The accuracy of the data must, of course, be considered within the context of daily risk factors experienced by the troops. The exposure to intense combat, sleep deprivation, the length of tours, and poor officer and NCO leadership were associated with increased mental health issues among them. Similarly,

NCOs who experienced multiple deployments, with potentially repeat exposures to these risk factors, experienced significantly higher rates of mental health issues than did troops deploying for the first time.

In general in these surveys, at least within the initial round of data analysis, troops that reported mental health issues were twice as likely to report engaging in noncompliant behavior toward civilians. In particular, those who reported high levels of anger were seven times more likely to report unnecessarily physically striking civilians than were those with low anger levels. Unit leaders might be able to take steps to mitigate exposure to intense combat feelings of rage through troop rotation policies, and they might be able to encourage sleep cycle discipline without increasing troops' consumption of sleep medications. They might also be able to promote the use by their troops of resources such as the Combat Stress Teams composed of behavioral health personnel used by US military in Afghanistan starting in 2009, if these sorts of resources are practicably available.[64]

Protective factors

Small unit commanders and NCOs, however, will not be able to influence tour length. Nor will they be free of the exigencies of the operational tempo, driven in significant part by those who would already wish to do them and their soldiers harm. The quality of their leadership, on the other hand, is something over which they have direct control.

Because quality leadership is such an important protective feature, it must be protected itself. Attention needs to be paid to training company-grade commanders on IHL, to make them more effective role models for their subordinate leaders. Special attention must be paid to junior NCOs, who are the leaders closest to the troops. Those with multiple combat deployments appear more susceptible to mental health issues, and even if there is no causal relationship between mental health issues and IHL violations, it is not likely they can serve as the best role models for their troops if they are already bearing a disproportionate load of stress. More extensive IHL training, perhaps in discussion or seminar formats, would respect the outsized role they play in keeping troops IHL-compliant and continue to develop them as leaders.

Summary

The mental health surveys conducted of US troops in Afghanistan and Iraq stand out as comprehensive assessments of the mental well-being of combat personnel and the factors that influenced those states of health. What is truly remarkable about the MHAT IV Iraq and the MHAT V surveys, however, are the ethical attitude and behavior questions that were asked of the respondents, which are closely correlated with issues of IHL compliance by the troops in combat. It must have taken significant political courage for the US military leaders at the time to authorize these unprecedented questions. Perhaps the decision to do so in the MHAT IV and MHAT V Iraq surveys reflected the very grave operational situation the US and coalition forces faced in Iraq at that time and a willingness to try new approaches that could help reverse the flow of the conflict. Regardless, asking soldiers who are in combat about their perceptions, attitudes, and behaviors within the context of a medical survey, rather than asking them directly about their compliance with IHL, likely elicited more honest, and therefore more useful, answers.

In correlating their answers, it is important to note the differences between their responses to the hypothetical questions asked about whether they would report comrades for IHL violations as compared to whether they themselves had committed even relatively less serious IHL infractions. There is an important delta here—while the majority of the respondents would not report even serious violations by others, they themselves largely maintained their self-discipline and did not engage in such acts. This reservoir of self-discipline could be tapped in useful ways to foster in trained soldiers the internalization of complementary IHL principles.

The survey responses showed troubling consistencies both within the same operational theater year to year (Iraq) and across operational theaters (Afghanistan and Iraq) regarding the likelihood of noncompliance with some of the bedrock implementing principles of IHL, such as reporting IHL violations.[65] These surveys showed that soldiers' mental well-being has direct and indirect impacts on attitudes and behaviors related to IHL compliance, and that repeated combat deployments, the degree of combat exposure, and lack of sleep are risk factors to be considered in maintaining their mental health. Helpfully though, these surveys also established that high-quality leadership, from both officers and NCOs, is a protective factor. It is plausible that efforts to increase the quality and intensity of IHL education and training would help with leader development and could therefore indirectly influence the command climates of units in positive ways beyond just increasing knowledge about IHL.

To put the results of these surveys into context, it is important to note that the advisory team registered an important caveat regarding the responses to the ethical attitude and behavior questions. It recognized that "one of the potential limitations associated with interpreting the ethics questions is that it was necessary to use un-validated scales. As such, there are no established norms upon which to help interpret the items."[66] While this is likely true from a research perspective, it is certainly not true from either a commander's or an IHL command responsibility perspective.

The MHAT IV report set out four recommendations to address the problems the survey had revealed in this regard. One recommendation was to the US Army and US Marine Corps commands that were responsible for developing training and doctrine—"Develop Battlefield Ethics Training based on the 'Soldiers' Rules,' using [Iraq]-based scenarios so [troops] know exactly what behaviors are acceptable on the battlefield and the exact procedures for reporting violations."[67] Although the premise of this recommendation was not completely sound, because the issue does not actually appear to have been ignorance of the applicable standards, the proposal to conduct the remedial training in the combat theater was creative. It does not appear, however, that the US-based commands to which the recommendation was directed ever acted upon it.

By late 2007, however, the command in Iraq decided to take action. A multidisciplinary team led by military mental health professionals was tasked to create a training package to be given to troops already deployed there to see whether a different approach to ethical training could generate attitudes and behaviors that were more IHL-compliant. As described in the next chapter, the training investment that was then made to modify those negative attitudes and behaviors among many of the respondent troops even as they were fighting was both significant and very innovative. Most importantly, the training program's dividends were nothing short of remarkable.

Chapter 4

BATTLEFIELD ETHICS TRAINING IN IRAQ

Data from the MHAT IV and MHAT V surveys of US troops in Iraq showed a consistent and very troubling pattern of combat attitudes and behaviors related to the application and enforcement of IHL. In late 2007 the commander of Multinational Division-Center in Iraq, which was responsible for an area including Baghdad, ordered his staff to create and conduct "a battlefield ethics training program for all soldiers under his command." With the assistance of military legal and medical specialists, as well as civilian experts in ethics, the staff quickly created a lean curriculum grounded in IHL, the official US Army values, and the US Military Academy Honor Code.[1]

The battlefield ethics training program was innovative in three important ways. First, it was developed largely in Iraq, rather than being a product of training and doctrine organizations back in the United States. The second innovative factor was the method of delivery, particularly for units engaged in combat. All leaders in the division, from senior officers all the way down to the squad and team-level units in each company, were required to use the lesson plan with their immediate subordinates, who then taught it to their subordinates, a so-called chain teaching approach.[2] Third, the battlefield ethics training program was designed from the beginning to include data collection and analysis to determine whether its delivery actually resulted in changes in attitudes and behaviors of the troops trained regarding IHL.[3]

As shown by that data, the resulting changes in soldiers' attitudes and behaviors related to IHL were marked. In the time since this program was conducted, however, the US Army appears to have largely stayed on a track of IHL instruction for troops that largely gives responsibility for this work to its military attorneys, and perhaps still reflects the institutional scarring resulting from the maltreatment of detainees at Abu Ghraib. After reviewing the design and results of the battlefield ethics program, this chapter will examine the implementation of this approach and the incomplete steps the US Army has taken to effectively factor the concept of honorable professionalism into the way IHL training is designed and delivered. Finally, important American legal scholarship on the use of empirical methods assessing the effectiveness of IHL education and training in operations will be reviewed. Altogether, this will highlight some of the larger gaps that should be addressed to make the US Army's approach more effective, including the need for empirical analysis.

Battlefield Ethics Training Program Design

Although the training was given to all troops in the Multinational Division-Center, the program developers focused on one BCT, approximately 3,500 soldiers, in conducting the surveys of the program's impact on attitudes and behaviors. First, an anonymous pretraining survey was conducted, and it included all the BCT soldiers who had participated in the MHAT V Iraq survey.[4] This commonality in participants likely made it easier to later draw conclusions about the strengths of relationships between the data that had prompted the training program and the data collected from the respondents after the training had been conducted. When the MHAT V Iraq survey was taken, the BCT soldiers had been in theater between three and four months.[5]

Then, about three months after the training had been conducted, a follow-up survey was administered. In addition to demographic questions and questions related to exposure to combat and mental health, both surveys included the original questions asked in the MHAT V Iraq survey relevant to IHL compliance, as well as nine new questions "to assess the training and factors associated with unethical conduct." For the posttraining survey, 421 of the 500 soldiers who were chosen at random and asked to participate completed and submitted the questionnaires. These were largely male enlisted soldiers who were on their first deployment.[6]

Based on feedback from the MHAT V Iraq survey focus groups, the chain teaching program was built to emphasize leader interaction with their troops and to avoid reliance on the typical PowerPoint IHL briefings they ordinarily received. From the division commander down, successive levels of leaders taught their immediate subordinates until every soldier in the division had received the instruction. The training was purposefully designed to occur in small groups, so that those soldiers who served together could engage in discussion.

The teaching curriculum was loaded onto compact discs, and it used video clips from certain movies to provide a common experiential learning basis among the small groups. A few traditional PowerPoint slides were included to help provide a basic structure for the training delivery. A script was also provided to ensure a level of standardized instruction despite the large number of actual leader instructors, and the scripts included key questions and discussion points for each of the video clips. The leaders were encouraged to depart from the script, however, and to tailor their presentations to actual events and problems that their units had experienced.[7]

Training Program Content

The training was expected to take between 60 and 90 minutes to complete. In their introductions of the program, the leader instructors explained to their troops the key points of the Army values, the 10 Soldier's Rules, and basic IHL principles. As will be discussed in greater detail later in this chapter, the 10 Soldier's Rules are a list of actions set out by US Army regulation for soldiers to either take or avoid in armed conflict to remain compliant with IHL. Importantly, the lead instructors also directly addressed the "Why?" of the training (the troubling results of the MHAT V Iraq report) and flags for potential misconduct. The movie clips were geared toward five themes: proper treatment of those not in combat; avoiding looting and pillaging; proper treatment of the wounded; prohibited killing of those not in combat; and reporting ethical violations. The longest clip was under four minutes long.[8]

The clips were generally from popular US war films, and therefore some of the soldiers had likely already seen them. For example, the movie clip supporting the discussion theme of treatment of noncombatants was from the film *Platoon*, a 1986 film that won four Academy awards[9] and was selected for preservation in the Library of Congress' National Film Registry for its cultural and aesthetic significance.[10] The clip was described as showing a "unit searching a village immediately following a significant engagement." The main discussion points the leader instructors were required to cover were "coping with stress, balancing excessive versus prudent force, Rules of Engagement, and preventing maladaptive stress induced responses." The warning flags discussed "included cursing, destroying property for no reason, or killing of animals."[11]

Importantly, the discussion points were not solely about misbehavior; they also reinforced positive messages as well. For example, in discussing the theme of reporting ethical violations, soldiers were reminded that it was important to understand that "investigations after combat incidents are not just about determining wrong-doing but are also about providing reassurance that the proper steps and actions are taken and garnering the lessons that can be learned." The curriculum also noted that there were protective factors that helped avoid violations, including good leadership, high levels of unit cohesion, and adequate sleep. These ideas were likely reinforced through the chain teaching method that made one group's students the instructor leaders for their immediate subordinates.[12]

Training Results

Mental health issues

An analysis of survey results showed that the pretraining and posttraining groups of respondents were comparable in terms of demographics, concerns regarding mental health, and amounts of time they had spent outside the protection of their bases each week. As to mental health, more than 20 percent of the posttraining survey respondents reported they experienced depression or PTSD, roughly the same as the pretraining respondents. As expected, the posttraining group had higher levels of different types of combat experiences, given the time that had elapsed since the pretraining survey. Only one of the soldiers who met the criteria for PTSD reported no combat exposure during their deployment.[13]

The training program team did identity one result that contrasted with those from the initial analysis of the MHAT V survey results that had explored the relationship between PTSD and physically striking civilians. Once the variables of positive screenings for PTSD or depression, spending more than 20 hours a week outside the base, and high-intensity combat were combined with demographic variables, there was no significant relationship between PTSD and unnecessarily hitting or kicking civilians. At worst, it was only a weak predictor of yelling or cursing at them.[14]

Changes in attitudes and behaviors

The changes in the attitudes and behaviors shown by the posttraining surveys were remarkable. All the answers regarding the adequacy of training, soldiers' actual behaviors and experiences while they were deployed, and their attitudes toward IHL-compliant conduct showed marked improvement over the pretraining survey results, and in many cases, these differences were statistically significant. The number of soldiers who had encountered ethical situations in which they did not know how to respond decreased by 62.7 percent. The number of soldiers who had unnecessarily damaged civilian property or who had witnessed unit members mistreating those not in combat decreased by similar amounts, 63.2 and 66.2 percent, respectively.[15]

Similarly, the changes in soldiers' attitudes as to when they would report comrades for IHL violations or for violating orders on the use of force were all positive, and all statistically significant. For example, the number of soldiers who would report a comrade for mistreating a person not in combat rose 63.6 percent. Similar results were found for reporting instances of stealing from noncombatants and violating ROE, 67.4 and 66.2 percent, respectively.

Those who would report unit members for unnecessarily damaging civilian property increased 80.0 percent. Interestingly, the number of soldiers who would now report a comrade for injuring or killing a person not in combat was also a statistically significant improvement, but still represented only a 54.8 percent increase.[16]

Soldiers' assessment of the training

The questions geared toward assessing the quality and effect of the training program provide important information for IHL instructors and, when compared to the questions regarding attitudes and experiences, arguably suggest that the program was more effective than the soldiers gave it credit for. For example, only slightly over half of the respondents found that the chain teaching method was an effective way to teach ethics, and unfortunately 58.4 percent believed that the training gave them the impression that the command thought all soldiers were committing ethical violations. As to the value of the movie clips, only slightly more than half agreed that they were useful in better understanding the points that were discussed in the training.[17] This result is fairly similar to the 35 percent of CGSC survey respondents, noted in Chapter 2, who had found video clips to be effective for IHL training.

Three questions, however, generated positive responses regarding the training above the rate of 60 percent. 60.3 percent agreed that the training clearly showed the impact of IHL violations on the mission, 62.0 percent agreed that it clearly showed how their leaders expected them to react when confronted with ethical dilemmas in combat, and 62.3 agreed that they had learned the proper steps to take if they witnessed a violation. Further, the training program team conducted subgroup analyses to determine whether PTSD, time spent operating outside the base, or combat exposure impacted the way the soldiers perceived the training. No significant differences or trends were found. Importantly, although roughly a third of the respondents were consistently neutral on each question (a finding worth further exploration itself), only between 3.8 and 6.7 percent were negative on the value and effects of the training.[18]

The significance of combat exposure

Another important finding of the posttraining survey was that combat exposure was the only significant predictor of physical mistreatment of civilians. The training team found that it correlated with anecdotal descriptions by combat veterans of intense rage in association with traumatic events such as losing a close comrade. The training team also recognized that those who spent more than 20 hours per week outside their bases averaged a greater number of combat exposures than those who did not, and they likewise would also interact more frequently with civilians. Although it was a different war, these findings are consistent with a study conducted on 1,104 US Army and US Marine Corps veterans of the Vietnam War, which found that "the factor that played the greatest role in predicting [involvement in] atrocities was combat exposure."[19] Accordingly, the Iraq training team recommended that battlefield ethics training should be a priority for those units that are expected to both engage in high-intensity combat and have the most interaction with civilians.[20]

The impact of leadership

Finally, the training team assessed that the single most important factor in the marked improvements in attitudes and behaviors was the "discussion by leaders that led to a cultural change in which unit awareness of ethical issues and leadership expectations improved."[21] Two of the training program's lead developers concluded that "as evidenced by the battlefield ethics training program, appropriate ethical performance is not achieved through a specific training program, but instead through integrated ethical training and most importantly *engaged leadership*."[22] With this conclusion in mind, it is useful to now turn to examining the approach the US Army has taken to training IHL since that time, and to assess the degree to which it incorporates the role of leadership and its attendant qualities of honor and professionalism as part of a values set that promotes IHL compliance.

The US Army Approach to IHL Training

To best place the US Army's IHL training approach in context, it is useful to first look at how the US Department of Defense conceptualizes the framework and goals of IHL compliance in general. In addition to protecting civilians and detainees and helping commanders use military force with discipline and efficiency, the United States also sees IHL as serving the vital purpose of "preserving the professionalism and humanity of combatants." The United States sees the IHL principles of military necessity, humanity, and honor as being interdependent and serving as a "foundation for other law of war principles, such as proportionality and distinction, and most of the treaty and customary rules of the law or war."[23]

The principle of honor and the professional ethos

Honor is a traditional IHL principle, and it was noted officially, for example, as a basis for restraint in the use of force in the Lieber Code that governed Union ground forces during the US Civil War.[24] However, as Judge Wallach has noted, honor (also called chivalry in the past[25]) has received little emphasis as an operative principle in the application of IHL in more recent times.[26] Today, the ICRC focuses on the principles of humanity, distinction, proportionality, and military necessity as the foundation of IHL—honor is not included.[27]

Despite this trend, the concept of honor factors significantly into the US Army's conceptualization of leadership and professionalism, and the expression of these fundamental ideas ties together with the principles and application of IHL. The US Army doctrine that covers these matters, *Army Doctrine Publication 6-22, Army Leadership and the Profession*, is intended for "all members of the Army profession, military and civilian. Trainers and educators throughout the Army will also use this publication." This reflects that the Army recognizes that leaders include NCOs and certain civilians as well as officers.[28]

The doctrine holistically defines the US Army professional ethic as "the set of enduring moral principles, values, beliefs, and laws that guide the Army profession and create the culture of trust essential to Army professionals in the conduct of missions, performance of duty, and all aspects of life." In implementing the US Army professional ethic, the doctrine describes effective leaders as having three fundamental traits: character, presence, and intellect.[29] For the purposes of creating a military culture that would foster effective IHL training, the most important of these traits is probably character.

Character is defined as having five components: Army values, empathy, warrior ethos and service ethos, discipline, and humility. Continuing with this hierarchical structure, there are seven Army values, including honor, integrity, and personal courage. Honor is defined as manifesting all the Army values, "set[ting] an example for every member of the organization and contribut[ing] to an organization's positive climate and morale." Integrity is defined as doing "what is right, legally and morally." Personal courage includes moral courage, which the doctrine defines as "the willingness to stand firm on values, principles, and convictions" and to be candid with others when expressing one's "carefully considered professional judgment."[30]

The professional ethos and IHL

This structure and content create a platform that is sufficiently developed to outline the presentation of IHL to US Army personnel as an integral part of a collective professional identity, one that could register both cognitively and emotionally. Importantly *Army Doctrine Publication 6-22* also specifically addresses the role played by IHL as part of the Army profession. As to the profession itself, the doctrine describes it as including honorable service, which is then described in part as follows:

> Soldiers in combat operations are responsible for the ethical application of lethal force in honorable service to the Nation. The law is explicit. Soldiers are bound to obey the legal and moral orders or their superiors; but they must disobey an unlawful or immoral order. Soldiers are also legally bound to report violations of the law of war to their chain of command.[31]

As to potentially illegal orders, US Army personnel are informed that if the issue is complex, they should seek legal counsel, but if they are in combat situation, they need to "make the best judgment possible based on the Army values, personal experience, critical thinking, previous study, and prior reflection." They are also directed to consult *Army Regulation 350-1*, which contains the 10 Soldier's Rules that "codify the law of war and outline ethical and lawful conduct in operations."[32] "Codify" is a bit of a misnomer; "list actions that comply with basic IHL requirements" is probably more accurate. Regardless, this work on its face seems to set out a conceptual structure that both establishes a platform for instruction on military professional ethics and describes linkages between the concept of honorable professionalism and IHL principles and instruction.

IHL training as set out in regulation

Unfortunately, this platform remains more of sketch than a useful blueprint for implementation. The reference to *Army Regulation 350-1* in the doctrinal publication on leadership is important, because this is the point where a very promising conceptual approach that includes IHL compliance as an important aspect of leadership and professionalism loses momentum when it actually comes to implementing it in education and training. Regarding the delivery of IHL training, as Jenks has concisely and accurately noted, this regulation has remained "curiously static,"[33] and it is largely unchanged since it was first promulgated in 2006—in part it appears to be a response to the atrocities committed by soldiers against detainees at Abu Ghraib.

The regulation designates the US Army Judge Advocate General as the executive authority for IHL training and tasks that officer with the development of the products that support IHL training across the force.[34] It sets out the basic content that these instructors are required to provide annually to units or prior to the units deploying, including the 10 Soldier's Rules and the basic rules applicable to the proper treatment of detainees and preventing their abuse. The 10 Soldier's Rules are pithy restatements of more complex IHL principles and concepts such as "Fight only enemy combatants" and "Treat all civilians humanely."

The significance of simplified rules like these in building a baseline of resilient moral decision-making among troops will be discussed in greater detail in Chapter 5. The regulation also requires instructors to tailor IHL training to mission requirements and locations and to integrate it into other unit training.[35] Beginning in 2006, the regulation also designated military attorneys and certified soldier paralegals as the instructors who were qualified to provide annual and predeployment training in IHL to units.[36]

This designation remains in effect today, and it is the military attorney or paralegal who is responsible for evaluating the soldiers' performance "using established training conditions and performance standards."[37] These performance standards are not further described, but because this level of training is a "reinforcement of the initial military training, along with detention training and mission-specific [IHL] training,"[38] the evaluation is not likely to involve an empirical assessment of efficacy in IHL application by the soldiers.

The approach the regulation outlines for providing basic instruction in IHL to soldiers is not unsound. Likewise, there is little question that the amount and quality of training the military attorney instructors and paralegals receive in addition to their ordinary legal training prepares them well for this role. Further, the central role that the US Army's Judge Advocate General's Law Center and School plays in both resourcing training and promoting uniformity of instruction throughout the US Army[39] very likely leads to a standard level of quality instruction in basic IHL across the force.

There are two very important elements missing here, however. First, there is no meaningful explanation of how these legal focus points link up with the moral and ethical concerns addressed in *Army Doctrine Publication 6-22*. Second, there is no reference to the role empirical assessment of the training could play in terms of evaluating the effectiveness of the training.

American Legal Scholarship on Empiricism and IHL Compliance

Although the US Army does not appear to appreciate the potential for empirical assessment of IHL training effectiveness, at least in terms of its doctrine and regulation, American IHL scholars have not ignored its importance. Hansen and Dickinson, in particular, have each contributed thoughtful and detailed studies to this literature.

The holistic use of data related to disciplinary proceedings and mental health

In 2008 Hansen proposed an empirical methodology to research IHL violations holistically, with an emphasis on data related to military discipline investigations and proceedings. His deep familiarity with the US military justice system allowed him to explain in detail the types of information that could be useful and how they might be used, but he also forthrightly noted potential challenges in collecting and analyzing this information.

The methodology's purpose focused on the crucial role of commanders in maintaining disciplined fighting forces in the field, enabling them to better understand occurrences of IHL violations through feedback designed to "assist them in developing effective IHL compliance mechanisms."[40] Pragmatically, Hansen identified a number of possible obstacles to this approach, including the exigent circumstances under which decisions that resulted in violations occurred, the difficulties of collecting evidence and testimony in fluid and unsecured combat environments, high personnel turnover in units, and the responsible units' "constant movements and changes in missions and taskings." Further, there could be issues with the accuracy of any information that was collected and concerns as to what it fully meant to the larger goal of better understanding the reasons why violations had occurred in the first place.[41]

Mindful of these challenges, Hansen argued that an empirical study "that recognize[d] a mosaic of techniques, sources, approaches and methodologies which can shed light on battlefield conduct" could prove feasible and useful. This mosaic would include military justice and disciplinary statistics, individual case studies involving IHL violations, data on investigations that did not result in the imposition of military discipline, changes in military doctrine related to IHL issues, and after-action reports and "lessons learned" studies.[42] This proposal could be fairly seen as a logical refinement of the norm enforcement approach set out in "The Roots of Behaviour in War" study, but Hansen did not stop there.

Importantly, his approach also recognized the value of assessments of troops' status outside the area of military discipline that were relevant to their attitudes and behaviors regarding IHL compliance. As an example of this, Hansen appreciated the significance of the data generated by the MHAT IV survey in Iraq, both in terms of troops' attitudes and behaviors related to IHL and the potential impact of their mental health on their feelings and actions. He favorably noted that the survey confirmed that good leadership played "an important role in maintaining a deployed service member's mental health and well-being."[43]

Military attorneys as compliance officers

The impact of good leadership also factored into Dickinson's 2010 study of military attorneys as IHL compliance officers. Consistent with the role carved out for US Army military attorneys in IHL training by regulation, Dickinson took an empirical approach to assessing the effectiveness of military attorneys advising commanders in the field. Her approach was based on what she saw as the role of military attorneys as organizational compliance officers within their units. From an organizational theory perspective, she noted research that suggested that within organizations, the "existence of a compliance unit, combined with the ability of compliance employees to report misconduct up a chain of command independent of the operational employee management chain, may enhance compliance."[44] Dickinson focused on US military attorneys, because she saw them as key to making sure that commanders and troops acted in compliance with their ROE.[45]

She had conducted her research in 2007 by first interviewing 20 military attorneys, the majority of whom had been deployed to Afghanistan or Iraq since 2002.[46] Importantly, this sampling places her interviewees as perhaps having deployed with units that the CGSC student survey respondents in Chapter 2 had recently commanded, but before the battlefield ethics training was conducted in Iraq in late 2007 and early 2008. Given that these initial interviewees were graduate students at The Judge Advocate General's Legal Center and School, most of them were likely relatively new majors themselves.[47]

Cautiously, Dickinson noted that her research was just one case study, and that it was likely her interviewees had overstated "their own importance as agents of compliance." She concluded, however, that "when we think about international law compliance, we cannot ignore organizational structure and institutional culture." Dickinson also assessed that the military attorneys were "most likely to function effectively and encourage legal compliance if certain organizational structures" were present, such as whether they were integrated into the units, and they had "a strong understanding of, and a sense of commitment to, the rules and values being enforced."[48]

Dickinson's caveats regarding the role of military attorneys in fostering IHL compliance in units appear to have been borne out in the investigations of Australian special forces troops in Afghanistan. The investigators whose work was relied upon in the Brereton Report suggested that some of the legal officers supporting the special forces units "drank the Kool-Aid." The investigators perceived that rather than recognizing that the Commonwealth of Australia was their actual client, they identified too closely with the troops being questioned and the unit itself, and thereby professionally conflicted themselves and hindered the investigations. Further, there was some concern that legal officers had not impartially reviewed complaints that had been filed against the special forces troops, thereby delaying the discovery of IHL violations. Lastly, certain "legal officers contributed to the embellishment of operational reporting, so that it plainly demonstrated apparent compliance with the rules of engagement." This too would have contributed to the chain of command not recognizing something was amiss in the conduct of operations.[49]

Whether directly or indirectly, both Hansen and Dickinson recognized the importance of the commander in IHL compliance in their respective approaches to empirical assessment. The rules and the values being enforced in a unit are strongly mediated by the command climate within the unit and the attitudes and actions of the unit commander.[50] In the US military, these things are regularly surveyed among the troops,[51] and the results of these surveys on leaders' careers can be very significant.[52] Further, the military establishments of allied countries, such as the United Kingdom and Australia, use similar assessment tools.[53] So, there is no institutional bias against empirical assessment of the effectiveness of intangible, human-oriented elements in these militaries and grounding important decision-making on this basis. It just does not seem to be done for IHL training. With this as background, consideration of the battlefield ethics training program and the US Army's approach to IHL training discloses important points that should be considered in creating, delivering, and measuring effective training.

Analysis

The battlefield ethics training program

There are three aspects of the battlefield ethics training program that deserve to be explored in greater detail. First, the results of the training program were briefed to senior US Army leadership[54] and publicized in well-read journals, so there must have been awareness of the improvements registered in the soldiers' attitudes and behaviors related to IHL. However, since that time, there appear to have been only small changes in the US Army's approach to IHL training in terms of leveraging the positive effects of leadership and professional military values, and no obvious change in terms of incorporating empirical assessment of training effectiveness into its IHL training.

Second, because of their work, the training program team was able to make important clarifications regarding the relationships between mental health issues and troop attitudes and behaviors that were not compliant with IHL.

Based on the MHAT V Iraq report, it appeared that there was a substantial correlation between mental health issues in general and IHL violations. The survey results from the battlefield ethics training program, however, suggested that this analysis was too broad, and that PTSD, for example, was not strongly associated with behaviors such as physical maltreatment of civilians like combat exposure was.[55]

A later secondary analysis of the MHAT V survey results largely substantiated the findings of the training program developers in this regard. Although PTSD was associated with unethical behavior, this association was not as strong as those between unethical behavior and aggression, time spent outside of the relative safety of bases, and particular combat experiences, such as witnessing atrocities. PTSD itself did not commonly result in unethical behavior.[56] In an even more granular assessment of the survey data, researchers subsequently concluded that "specific combat experiences are related to increased unethical battlefield conduct above and beyond having more time in the battlefield."[57]

A 2013 British study provides further context for these findings, and although the findings of this study are different in certain respects, they are not necessarily inconsistent with those of the American research. In this study, researchers reviewed the histories of 13,856 Britons who had served in the military in Afghanistan or Iraq, and who had experienced at least one conviction for criminal behavior during their lifetimes. They found that although deployment itself was not associated with an increased risk of violent offending, service in a combat role was an additional risk factor. Greater exposure to traumatic events while deployed also resulted in increased risk of committing a violent offense.[58]

Further, the researchers found a strong link between PTSD and committing violent offenses, and PTSD appeared to mediate the link between traumatic events and these acts. Importantly, they pointed out that PTSD manifests in different ways among different patients. The study authors noted research that had strongly linked the cluster of symptoms categorized by "irritability or outbursts of anger and alertness to threat," or hyperarousal, to violent behavior, and they found their results supported this finding.[59]

These analyses are useful for military leaders at all levels and IHL instructors to carefully consider in developing effective IHL training and delivering it timely. When giving IHL training while troops are deployed, the MHAT studies suggest that there is a point during the deployment when it could have the greatest effect. Similarly, at the unit level, experiencing traumatic combat events, such as the loss of a particularly well-liked comrade, are times when a tailored IHL training intervention might be most useful. In the same vein, soldiers should not be discouraged in seeking behavioral health care, and drawing too broad a connection between mental health issues in general and potential IHL violations is not just inaccurate; it risks further stigmatizing those who need this care to help them continue performing their duties well and in conformance with expected standards.

Third, the battlefield ethics training team concluded that what made the program successful was not the quality of the curriculum design, but instead the engagement of leaders at all levels with their subordinates on these important ethical and legal issues. This is a fair assessment. Consistent with militaries using training as a remedy for shortcomings, almost 60 percent of the respondents believed they had been given the training because they were all committing ethical violations. To be blunt, what this really meant and to be concerned about is that they felt they were being labeled as war criminals. These sorts of perceptions of IHL-related training likely create unnecessary emotional and cognitive barriers to delivering training that will be effective in the field. This may have colored the soldiers' assessment of the battlefield ethics training in general. Further, the post-training survey data did find that only about half of the soldiers surveyed found the leader-led chain teaching method to be effective, and only about half found the movie clips to be effective in the training. Logically then, there had to be some other factor that made the instruction so successful.

Importantly, it was the rigorous design of the training program that allowed the training team to be able to collect data that would allow them to make this sort of objective assessment of what worked and why. This was not likely appreciated by the soldier respondents—nor would it have been reasonable to expect them to. These results also showed that very few respondents had a negative view of the training. Over 60 percent agreed that they understood the impact of violations on the mission, that they understood what their leaders expected of them, and that they had learned the proper steps to take if they saw an IHL violation. These results are plausibly linked to leader engagement.

However, there was another factor that might also have been very significant that was not really addressed by the survey questions—the moral intensity of the instructional setting. This instruction was not merely academic for the leaders and soldiers; it was instead very real, in a very serious situation in an actual combat theater. As will be discussed in greater detail in the next chapter on different education and training case studies, realism and intensity have a way of focusing people's attention on the matter being trained.

The US Army approach to IHL training

To a significant degree, the US Army Judge Advocate General's Corps has sought to make IHL more accessible to commanders and to promote the role of commanders and values in ensuring IHL compliance by the troops. As one example, the Judge Advocate General's Legal Center and School has published the *Commander's Legal Handbook*, which identifies factors that have sometimes led to war crimes being committed, such as high unit casualties, poor training, and high levels of frustration among troops. It recommends that these factors be monitored, addressed by leaders, and included in training.[60] It does not, however, meaningfully explain how this is to be done.

Further, there appears to be a gap between the executive authority given to the US Army Judge Advocate General for IHL training by regulation and the handbook's description of who makes this training happen. Commanders are reminded that military attorneys can assist them in IHL training, but that they have the primary responsibility for ensuring their soldiers receive the training and establishing the specific training objectives.[61] Commanders, of course, control their units' training, but by regulation, the IHL training content and the instructors are largely prescribed. Surely there is a more important role for commanders in this regard than confirming the training objectives and deconflicting the training schedule—as Jenks has persuasively argued, "the unit leader should have the primary responsibility" for this training.[62]

The US Army Judge Advocate General's Corps is also the US Army proponent for *Field Manual 6-27, The Commander's Handbook on the Law of Land Warfare*, which helpfully distills the 1,236-page Department of Defense *Law of War Manual* down to a more manageable 206 pages.[63] Although it does not refer to honor with regard to IHL training, it does state that "honor is a core Army and Marine Corps value," and it defines honor as "a matter of carrying out, acting, and living out other core values, such as respect, duty, loyalty, selfless service, integrity, and personal courage, in everything Soldiers and Marines do." Specifically, the handbook also notes that "honor also requires adherence to [IHL] regardless of the enemy's level of compliance."[64] However, it likewise does not provide any roadmap on how to practically incorporate this information into training from a values perspective.[65]

Neither of these otherwise useful documents meaningfully elaborate on the conceptual scheme behind the role of leadership and the scope of the honorable professionalism associated with it in *Army Doctrine Publication 6-22, Army Leadership and the Profession*. Instead, in terms of practical application, what these publications set forth for IHL training places a heavy emphasis on instruction in the norms of IHL by the same organization that would in the event of a violation be responsible for providing the prosecutors and defense counsel in any disciplinary hearings. These books contain little guidance as to how to navigate between the training and its later application in the field and, therefore, how to better avoid the unsatisfying legal end point of IHL violations altogether.

This approach perhaps reflects the general assumption that Blank has identified as underlying many IHL tribunal decisions—IHL training results in IHL compliance.[66] One could argue that the low rate of IHL violations displayed by US troops in the wars fought since the Al Qaeda attacks in 2001 proves that the training scheme is effective. That argument is not without merit, but this presumption of causality could be tested by empirical assessment, as shown by the battlefield ethics training program in Iraq.

American legal scholarship on empirical assessment of IHL training

Hansen's and Dickinson's work in applying an empirical assessment perspective to IHL compliance provides an important foundation for the efforts to make IHL training more effective in protecting civilians and detainees. Hansen's holistic approach with its emphasis on the collection and analysis of disciplinary data, and Dickinson's organizational approach in seeking to quantify the impacts of military attorneys as IHL compliance officers in their units, both illustrate useful points for commanders and IHL instructors to consider in the creation and delivery of IHL training to troops. With their forthright discussions of the limitations of their respective approaches, these authors also provide cautions on using empirical approaches that are focused in substantial part on the enforcement, either formally or informally, of IHL.

To build on these points, it is important to first recognize that within countries' home audiences, there might be little stomach for criminal accountability of even troops that commit grave IHL violations if the public perceives the conflict in which they are fighting to be just. For example, one recent survey of US civilians showed that almost "half of respondents were willing to allow the massacre of innocent women and children to go unpunished when they believed the act was committed by soldiers fighting for a just cause" when presented with a hypothetical conflict situation.[67]

Second, as shown by President Trump's pardon in 2019 of US Army Lieutenant Lorance, who had been convicted of ordering his soldiers to kill two Afghan civilians,[68] and his pardons in 2020 of four US private military contractors who had been convicted in the killings of innocent Iraqi civilians,[69] the legal process in these cases can become highly politicized and the results of investigations and trials can be irrationally skewed by influences that have nothing to do with the facts of the violations. Sadly, as shown by President Nixon's 1971 order releasing Lieutenant Calley from confinement, who had been sentenced to life imprisonment for the murder of 22 civilians in the My Lai massacre in South Vietnam, and instead placing him under house arrest, the politicization of trials for offenses that are grave violations under IHL is not a new phenomenon for the United States.[70]

Third, even when cases get to trial, conviction is uncertain given the need to prove guilt beyond a reasonable doubt based on facts generated amid the chaos of armed conflict. For example, one assessment of US Army court-martial proceedings based on IHL violations between 2002 and 2012 found that 43 soldiers were tried as defendants, but only 28 were convicted, leading to an acquittal rate of more than twice that in regular courts-martial.[71] But there are complexities other than failures of proof that make the results of these cases uncertain metrics to use in assessing the effectiveness of IHL and IHL-related training, as demonstrated by the trial of a senior Royal Netherlands Marine Corps NCO in 2005 for alleged violations of his ROE that led to him shooting an Iraqi civilian and for the resulting negligent homicide.

As the NCO and his Marines were providing security for an overturned supply truck, a group of civilians apparently intent on looting the vehicle converged upon it. The NCO went through a quick series of escalation of force measures, which culminated in him firing a warning shot into the ground in front of the civilians, but off to the side. A civilian then fell to the ground wounded and later died. The pocket cards that set out the uses of force allowed by the Marines that had been distributed to them by their command did not specifically provide for the steps taken by the NCO.[72]

The prosecution appealed the NCO's acquittal at the trial level. The appeals court held that although the cards did not specifically authorize the force escalation measures that the NCO had taken to deter the looters, those steps were allowable under the ROE that had been authorized for the mission as a whole. Because the cards were subordinate to the ROE, and the ROE had the legal status of being standing orders, the NCO therefore acted consistent with his orders when he shot. As to the negligent homicide charge, the appeals court found that the NCO had not acted recklessly in firing his warning shot. This case was controversial in the Netherlands, and in 2010, the Dutch Military Penal Code was amended to exclude criminal liability for the use of force by military personnel consistent with their lawful duties and orders.[73]

Sorting through the layers of ROE, even though they must be consistent with IHL, is complex from a criminal law perspective. Hansen's cautions as to the potential limitations of using disciplinary information and trial results to assess IHL training effectiveness are sound from a US military justice perspective. Writing 10 years later, Margalit expanded on similar challenges from an international perspective in his assessment of the variety of investigation mechanisms used by different countries. In particular, he noted the wide range in practice by different nations in determining which civilian casualties require investigation, the actual standards that are used to conduct the investigations, and the different identities and roles of the persons or organizations conducting the investigations and developing the reports of their findings.[74] Criminal justice data should be considered in developing an effective IHL training curriculum, but from both a moral and a practical perspective, it is simply more effective to avoid the need for criminal discipline related to IHL violations from the beginning.

Summary

The battlefield ethics training program conducted in Iraq in 2007 and 2008 showed that even in a combat zone, it is possible to deliver a multidisciplinary approach to IHL training that can efficiently reach troops and result in measurable, positive changes in their attitudes and behaviors related to IHL. Although there is a bias in IHL that legal advisors lead such instruction, the results of the program show that lawyers overseeing these efforts is not necessary to achieve positive results. Further, by taking a multidisciplinary approach to this training program, its authors were also able to gather important information regarding the impact of mental health and risk factors such as combat exposure on soldiers' attitudes and behaviors regarding IHL.

With its emphasis on instruction being conducted by leaders at all levels, its inclusion of values rather than just legal norms as part of the curriculum design, and its focus on data collection and analysis from the very beginning, this training program was very innovative. As Mastroanni has noted regarding the reciprocal relationships between attitudes and behaviors, "if you want to change behavior, then one way is to change attitudes. As it happens, a good way to change attitudes is to change behavior."[75] The battlefield ethics training program changed the behavior of leaders at all levels in the division by requiring them to engage with IHL issues with their subordinates. An effect of this was likely the changes in attitudes and behaviors noted in the post-training survey respondents.

Recently, Jenks has pointed out that the most recent version of the official directive that establishes the US military's IHL program now requires that it be "effective."[76] However, the directive contains no guidance on how efficacy should be defined or the metrics to be used in assessing it.[77] Regrettably, there is no evidence in doctrine or regulation that the innovative approach to effective IHL instruction demonstrated by the battlefield ethics training program has been scaled up for use across the US Army.

Similarly, US Army doctrine on leadership and the military profession provides a decent conceptual platform on which to create IHL training that relates to values that the organization wants to instill in its members that would foster a positive collective identity of honorable professionalism. The supporting doctrine and guidance that is closest to the actual implementation of IHL training, however, does not provide commanders or IHL instructors with meaningful pathways to establish these linkages. Further, none of this doctrine addresses the value that empirical assessment could bring in focusing IHL training to make sure that it is both efficient and effective.

From an assessment perspective, the work of American IHL scholars setting out different approaches to measure IHL compliance is valuable in exploring the advantages and the disadvantages of approaches that are largely geared to examining data related to formal and informal IHL enforcement. These approaches face certain complexities, not the least of which are the difficulties in establishing causality between the training given and the things that would be measured to assess performance. In sum, metrics need to be developed and applied to measure the potential for performance closer to the education and training itself. With this in mind, let us turn now to Chapter 5, which explores several additional case studies from across the world that have creatively used empirical assessment as an integral part of IHL or IHL-related education and training in this manner.

Chapter 5

EDUCATION AND TRAINING
CASE STUDIES

In the years since the training intervention staged by the divisional command in Iraq in 2007 and 2008, different researchers, instructors, and commanders have continued to include empirical assessment in the IHL and IHL-related curricula and programs they have developed. This chapter looks at five examples of this kind of education and training, which all took very different approaches to instruction with very different groups of students. In addition to the use of empirical assessment, the other elements that these case studies have in common are innovation and the careful tailoring of the individual programs to their respective audiences. These similarities are sufficient to make many of the positive points, and the limitations identified in each, more broadly applicable across a range of IHL education and training programs, and worthwhile for any curriculum development team to consider if they want to know quantitatively at the end whether their investment has been worthwhile.

The first case study is of Norwegian military academy cadets whose moral reasoning skills were tested in a rested state and then in a sleep-deprived state during combat simulation training. The second case study is of young Swiss officers in a stable, well-resourced academic environment learning moral decision-making techniques by using scenarios that posed realistic ethical dilemmas of varying moral intensity. The third is of new Malian soldiers learning IHL and related principles in an austere training environment in which they were preparing for imminent deployment to combat operations. The fourth is of US officers and NCOs in a battalion in a garrison environment that developed an extensive leadership development program that included IHL principles and leveraged the availability of nearby historical sites with strong IHL and human rights connections in conducting its capstone exercise.

The fifth kind of education and training, using war video games, must be considered in parallel with the innovative and proactive approaches the ICRC is now taking in working with the war video game industry. The potential for training young troops on IHL in a medium they enjoy is enormous, and a virtual world created by data likely lends itself to efficiently capturing data related to IHL-related attitudes and behaviors. This chapter concludes by looking at assessments conducted in two recent case studies based on university students playing variations of a popular war video game that purposefully included IHL content and play. These two studies, one from Northern Ireland and the other from Japan, illustrate both the potential of using these games for IHL education and training and the need to understand the technological and ethical complexities of virtual learning with these tools.

The Impact of Sleep Deprivation on Moral Decision-Making Skills

Moving from unethical behavior in general to the role of morals and morality in IHL compliance and enforcement might be seen by some as a rather large jump. In fact, a number of prominent IHL writers have criticized decisions of international tribunals that have incorporated aspects of morality in their evaluation of IHL violations, rather than relying on established legal principles.[1] On the other hand, from the perspective of ethics, other writers have pointed out that decisions made in the course of armed conflict have fundamental moral components and impacts.[2] Accordingly, many countries have integrated military ethics and moral decision-making into the training and education they provide their armed forces, and for this reason, the next two case studies are quite relevant to the larger question of the effectiveness of IHL training.[3]

Although it did not concern IHL education or training specifically, in 2010 a group of Norwegian researchers published a study on the effects of sleep deprivation on the moral reasoning methodologies used by Norwegian military academy cadets as they participated in combat simulation training. Certain research has suggested that a reduced amount of sleep may lead to unethical conduct. For example, in a study conducted with undergraduate students at a large US university, participants were given the opportunity and an incentive to cheat on an online quiz. Approximately 10 percent did so. The researchers found that participants being male and having reduced amounts of sleep the night before taking the quiz were the factors strongly associated with cheating on the quiz.[4]

The Norwegian training audience comprised 50 first-year officer cadets at the Norwegian Army Academy and 42 at the Royal Norwegian Naval Academy. All cadets already had at least one year of military service prior to entering the academies, and their mean length of service was 2.8 years. Their mean age was 24.2 years.[5]

The study was structured so that the cadets' moral reasoning methodologies were evaluated in both a rested state outside of combat simulation exercises and in a sleep-deprived state during the exercises. To control for circadian rhythm variations, the data in the rested state was collected between 0730 and 0830 in the morning, and the data in the sleep-deprived state was collected between 0430 and 0530. In each data collection, the cadets assessed their relative degree of sleepiness on a seven-point scale that ranged from 1 point ("feeling active, vital, alert or wide awake") to 7 points ("no longer fighting sleep, sleep onset soon, having dreamlike thoughts").[6]

The substantive part of the study required each cadet in both the rested and sleep-deprived states to resolve five moral dilemmas. For each dilemma, the cadets were presented with 12 arguments and asked to rank the four arguments they believed were of greatest importance to them in making their decisions. These rankings indicated the level of their preferred moral reasoning styles in making their decisions. The scores would fall within one of three styles: post-conventional (or principled, the highest level), conventional (maintaining norms, or rules-based), or personal interest (preconventional or self-serving moral thinking).[7]

Principled moral reasoning incorporates a social perspective and the ability to factor the equities of different stakeholders into moral judgments. "This capacity is highly vulnerable to lack of sleep."[8] The researchers found that there was a significant decrease in the use of principled moral reasoning among the cadets while in a sleep-deprived state, and a significant increase in the use of rules-based thinking, which is less complex than principled moral reasoning. Interestingly, there was no significant increase in the use of self-serving thinking in the sleep-deprived state.[9]

The researchers recognized the operational significance of their findings. While the moral reasoning skills of sleep-deprived officers in stressful conditions might be degraded, they would not necessarily "regress into pure self-centeredness when faced with moral challenges that may involve the life and welfare of others." The researchers appreciated the value of ROE and standard operating procedures "as simplified rules for making decisions in complex operational scenarios," because these measures incorporated moral judgments and concerns that might still "provide a basis for sound moral judgment" even if higher-level reasoning skills were degraded.[10]

Military Ethics and Moral Decision-Making Training

Although it likewise did not concern IHL education or training specifically, in 2011 a group of Swiss researchers published a case study on moral decision-making training for Swiss officers that was very thoroughly constructed and which captured useful information on both the effectiveness of the training and the collection of the data itself. In contrast to the Norwegian study, the participants in this study were not subjected to unusual physical stress. The study was conducted in a more traditional military academic atmosphere, largely in a classroom setting.

The training audience was composed of a total of 130 officers. The 46 officers in the intervention group were enrolled in an officers training program at the Swiss Military Academy in Zurich and had a mean age of 28.39 years. The control group consisted of 86 captains and majors from two command and staff courses for Swiss militia officers. These officers were comparable to the intervention group, although they tended to be a bit older, with a mean age of 31.41 years.[11] By way of comparison, as noted in Chapter 2, the average age of the US officers in the CGSC Class of 2002 was probably between 36 and 37 years. Twenty officers from the intervention group participated in the posttraining program effectiveness evaluation.[12]

The training took place over the course of five days, with six hours of instruction each day. The instruction mixed work on six real-life moral dilemmas with theoretical teaching on military ethics, leadership ethics, moral psychology, and the "individual, organizational, and contextual challenges related to moral behavior in the military profession."[13] The scenarios were based on real-life experiences of officers from different nations who had been involved in international peacekeeping operations.[14] The training cycled through five phases for each dilemma scenario.

In the first phase, the officers were introduced to a moral dilemma that was consistent with what they might encounter in their current or future work situations. In the second phase, the officers were given a predefined set of questions in advance and then asked to develop individual solutions to the dilemma using the structure of the questions as a guide.[15] For the third phase, the officers discussed their solutions in a small group setting. Then, in the fourth phase, each group was required to determine what they considered to be the best single solution. Finally, in the fifth phase, the different groups shared their solutions with each other.[16]

On the first day, the researchers gathered pretraining test data by presenting each of the intervention group participants with two moral dilemmas based on real-life experiences of other Swiss Army soldiers and then requiring them to compose a short essay that explained how they evaluated the situation and described a potential solution. The posttraining test data was collected in two tranches, the first on the last day of training, and the second six months later. In both instances, the officers were again presented with two real-life moral dilemmas and asked to solve them.[17]

Two raters then reviewed the responses independently, without knowing at what stage of the assessment they had been collected. The raters used a predetermined set of criteria that assessed both the content and process elements of the responses.[18] On the basis of their evaluation, the researchers assessed that the program's training approach had a significant positive effect on both content- and process-related moral decision-making competencies.[19] Six months later, the moral decision-making reasoning used by the officers still scored significantly higher on the evaluation criteria than the reasoning they used in the pretraining evaluation, although it had decreased from the quality of the reasoning shown in the test taken at the end of the course.[20]

When the researchers drilled deeper into the data related to content, they made a very interesting finding. In responding to the moral dilemmas with lower "moral intensity," that is, with a lesser magnitude of harm, the officers tended to not employ their moral decision-making competencies to their fullest extent. Accordingly, the researchers found that for individuals, an accurate assessment of their decision-making skill levels must "be based on decision-making behavior in high-stake situations."[21] This is consistent with a 2017 Dutch case study of a training program for instructors of military ethics that found what the participants remembered most were the realistic and challenging dilemmas their fellow students had experienced.[22] If these findings may be validly translated to assessing IHL training effectiveness, this suggests that training developers must find ways to introduce a level of stress and risk into their curricula and devote assessment resources to those strategic stress and risk points to determine how the training is actually registering on the training audience.

When looking into the data related to process, the researchers made another interesting finding. The officers were all, of course, familiar with applying structured problem-solving methodologies to military situations. In the pretraining test, however, they did not apply a structured approach to moral decision-making—this only happened after they had undergone the training program.[23] Although these results are the only sample to work with because the Swiss Military Academy does not appear to have used this moral decision-making program again,[24] if the results do validly translate to IHL training, they should give commanders and IHL instructors pause. Just because soldiers might be adept at applying structured reasoning to complex tactical problems does not mean that these skills lend themselves to resolving complex ethical or moral dilemmas, including those that involve IHL. Instead, specific training in application is likely required even for otherwise well-trained and educated troops.

Basic IHL Training in a Challenging Training Environment

Between 2013 and 2014, an instructor with the civil society organization Beyond Peace,[25] along with adjunct instructors from the United Nations and the ICRC, developed and delivered an IHL curriculum that included assessment to four battalions of Malian troops, about 2,700 in total.[26] In contrast to the Swiss officers who had received the moral decision-making training while they were students at a military school, these soldiers were being trained for imminent combat with insurgent forces in the north of the country. Further, for the most part, these soldiers were illiterate, and although many knew some French, they did not otherwise all share any common languages.[27]

To create a curriculum that would be most effective given the austerity of the training environment and the challenges posed by the training audience, the lead instructor worked through four developmental steps. First, she researched the cultural context that the troops lived in, including Malian history, national law, the impact of ethnicity, ethical standards and religion, education, learning styles, and how the troops related to authority. Next, she familiarized herself with the Malian Army's mission and its operations, as well as reports that identified what problems related to IHL the troops were experiencing in the field. Third, once she had developed this background, she pulled the basic principles from IHL, international human rights law, and law combating sexual violence from different legal authorities that were most pertinent to the problems that needed to be addressed. Finally, she worked to combine this all into a basic package that could be translated into uniform and accurate instruction.[28]

Over a period of 10 weeks, the troops received between one and two hours of classroom instruction per week in IHL and human rights. The instruction was delivered in a mixture of ways. This included presentations using PowerPoint when electricity was available and the use of charts printed on large tarpaulins and hung in the class area when training was conducted in the field. The course emphasized interaction with the troops, sometimes using them as role players during class, and by using sand table exercises to have them explain how they would implement IHL principles in conducting operations.

As much as possible, rather than just set out IHL and human rights principles as somewhat abstract international norms, the curriculum content sought to find linkages between these principles and local values, including Malian law, religion when appropriate, and professionalism. For example, the troops were not just taught about the legal principle of distinction between combatants and protected noncombatants. In addition, the concept was repurposed to explain from a perspective of professionalism the differences between what it meant to be a soldier rather than a bandit in the application of this principle, and how that would contribute to winning the conflict.[29]

Assessment was an integral part of this curriculum design. In the first class, the instructors asked the troops a series of questions as a pretraining test, to which they would respond with a show of hands. These results were recorded, and in the last class, the students were asked the same questions again.[30] Although the results were a little rough given the survey method, and of course there was room for potential bias from peer pressure because of the way each soldier's answer was visible to his comrades, these assessments for each battalion at the end of the course showed a marked improvement at least in the knowledge of IHL. Importantly, at the end of the training, the soldiers were also asked directly what they had learned from the course. Across all four battalions, the troops were able to not only identify the IHL principles they had learned but also explain the impact of those principles in working with civilians and representing the Malian Army.[31]

The assessment did not stop there. The IHL instruction was just a small part of the tactical training the soldiers were undergoing as they prepared for their combat deployment. IHL themes were also incorporated into the tactical exercises conducted with the soldiers, which were observed by the lead instructor and who provided feedback to soldiers on their performance from an IHL perspective. Before they deployed, the soldiers were each given a small pocket-sized booklet that captured the most important points of the IHL instruction in a picture format they could understand. The lead instructor had contracted with a local press to design and publish this booklet using waterproof material, with cartoons that reminded the soldiers of these points.[32] Although it is not an assessment measure itself, if later consulted by the soldiers, this booklet would likely have provided a useful reinforcement of what they had learned and practiced in their tactical exercises.

Although she was not allowed to deploy with the soldiers on their missions to the north, the lead instructor coordinated with international and nongovernmental organization personnel in that area to receive information about any reported violations by the soldiers. There are, of course, limitations on the accuracy of information collected in this fashion, but in general, the number of reports and the gravity of reported violations decreased. Finally, the lead instructor was able to gather feedback from the soldiers in the first battalion that had received the IHL training when they returned from their deployment to the training site for further training. When debriefed, many of the soldiers told her that their IHL training had made a difference in the way that they behaved toward civilians and that the civilians had noticed. Not just were civil–military relations better, but in some instances, civilians had come to them with information about the insurgents the soldiers were fighting.[33]

Accordingly, there can be no excuse for not finding ways to include meaningful empirical assessment in even the most basic of IHL training. In other training that has been given to the Malian military over the years, Knowles and Matisek have pointed out there is a dearth of information regarding the effectiveness of the IHL and human rights instruction the troops received. Although the metrics they suggest to begin remedying this situation are largely measures of performance rather than effectiveness, their larger point is still valid—effective training of this nature is consistent with the values of professionalism that must be made manifest in the military for it to be able to operate within the rule of law on the battlefield.[34] Even if the collection methodology has limitations, so long as those limitations are honestly accepted, useful data that does not always meet the standards of statistical rigor can still be gathered, analyzed, and fruitfully cycled into the next training iteration.

IHL Training as Part of Leadership Development

The usefulness of even limited data regarding IHL training effectiveness is also shown in a case study involving a US Army battalion with companies stationed in Germany and Italy in 2017. The battalion commander assessed that his unit's existing leadership development program did not provide enough opportunities for his officers and NCOs to reflect upon and develop their ethical decision-making processes, or to think about how they would exercise these skills from moral, legal, and professional perspectives.[35] His staff developed a new leadership development program using the Nazi genocide of European Jews in World War II as its overarching theme and took a multidisciplinary approach that combined different instructional methods to explore the protection of civilians and detainees from IHL violations as first and foremost a leadership issue.[36]

The battalion's leadership development program was staged over a three-month period, with videoconferencing used to connect the leaders of remote companies with the rest of the battalion. The separate lessons generally lasted between one and two hours, and the battalion commander made sure to clear the unit's training schedule to allow it to meet this schedule. By way of introduction, the first lesson was based on a historical reading about the Holocaust, followed by a traditional lecture from a member of the program team who had expertise in Holocaust history.

The next lesson was on a specific case study of a reserve *Wehrmacht* infantry battalion in Occupied Belarus in 1941, whose battalion commander one day ordered his company commanders to kill all the Jews in their respective areas of operations. The case study focuses on leadership and values at the small unit level—one commander complied with the order immediately, the second commander considered it and refused, and the third commander sought to avoid carrying out the order until the battalion commander confirmed it in writing. He then directed the first sergeant to direct the executions.[37] Using videoconferencing, the case study lead author engaged in a discussion with the battalion leaders from a National Guard base in the United States.

The next three sessions involved a practical exercise. First, the battalion's servicing military attorney introduced the leaders to the Army regulation that governs how administrative investigations are carried out and explained how to write an effective investigation report and recommendations. Next, the case study lead author gave a presentation via videoconference on the linkages between leader ethics and ethical decision-making and provided the battalion leaders a written assignment that required them to write an investigation report and make recommendations on how they could improve their battalion's training program to avoid ethical tragedies like the one in the case study. Prior to the final lesson, the case study lead author provided written feedback on each report to the commander, who used this to provide individualized feedback to each of his leaders on their work.[38] The final videoconference was led by the commander, who shared the points he had learned from reading the investigation reports, and how those linked with his leadership philosophy.[39]

The most important part of the leadership development program, however, was the staff ride that the battalion organized a couple of weeks later to visit the Nazi extermination camp that had been established in Occupied Poland at Auschwitz, with a stopover in Nuremberg to visit the Palace of Justice where the International Military Tribunal trials were held after World War II. The battalion leaders stayed at Auschwitz for two days, taking extended guided tours through areas of the complex, participating in seminars coordinated through the memorial site curators, and visiting nearby museums. At night, the battalion chaplain led reflection sessions with the leaders, addressing the difficult and emotional experiences they encountered during their visit.[40]

To assess the impact of the leadership development program on his subordinate leaders, the battalion commander had the chaplain conduct an anonymous online survey of the participants a couple of weeks after the staff ride. Slightly over half of the participants (40) responded to the survey, and about three-quarters were officers. Sixty-nine percent agreed that because of the program their understanding of IHL principles had improved. Eighty-five percent agreed that they were now more aware of different approaches they could use in making sound ethical decisions and of the impacts of their ethical decisions on their peers and subordinates. Ninety-two percent found the use of the "Ordinary Soldiers" case study was "sufficient or largely sufficient to understand the challenging ethical circumstances in which the German battalion commander had placed his company commanders."[41]

The staff ride to Auschwitz and Nuremberg was seen by 82 percent of the respondents as the most significant part of the leadership development program, the part that had the deepest personal impact upon them. Eighty percent found the site visits improved their understanding of the impacts of leaders making flawed ethical decisions, and 82 percent found that the visits had improved their understanding of their obligations as leaders to set and enforce value-driven standards. Perhaps most importantly, 92 percent of the respondents agreed that the program had increased unit cohesion.[42] A better-designed survey, of course, would have asked the training participants before the program their assessment of unit cohesion and then compared that with their answers to the same open-ended question in the postprogram survey, but overall the survey findings suggest that the leadership development program was viewed favorably by the battalion's officers and NCOs.

Incorporating IHL Training in War Video Game Play

Moving from real-world sites of mass atrocities to the virtual world of first-person shooter war video games, the ICRC has recognized both the challenges and the opportunities posed by war video game play in terms of promoting IHL compliance. Already, over the past few years, the ICRC has been using detailed video simulations with different national militaries that allow training participants to apply their understandings of IHL to operations that they have planned and to see what the effects of their actions would be.[43] The ICRC has also established its own laboratory in Bangkok to develop war video games that include IHL content and rules,[44] and it has also sought to constructively engage with the war video game industry to have IHL content and rules included in commercial products.[45]

The ICRC's efforts have led to a successful collaboration with Bohemian Interactive, the war video game developer that developed the commercially successful first-person shooter *Arma* game series. Bohemian Interactive created a special IHL downloadable content module called "Laws of War" for its *Arma 3* game, which provides opportunities for players to interact with a humanitarian group and to engage in peaceful (but dangerous) activities such as mine detection and clearing. It also contains a game that allows players to learn IHL rules and then practically apply them to the scenarios involving those not in combat.[46]

The scenarios do not prevent misuse of weapons, an ethical complexity of which the ICRC is aware, but the ICRC has decided that on balance it is acceptable that there will be some players who purposefully do so. The chief executive officer of Bohemia Interactive has been heartened by the support the module has received from the player community.[47] As noted in Chapter 1's discussion of the ICRC's recognition of the role these games might play in the education and training of young troops, however, the ethical concerns related to this style of play have not yet been resolved.

Arma 3 was the vehicle for two case studies in using war video games in a civilian academic environment. The first study, starting in 2015, was based on the results of using the video game and independently created interactive scenario modifications to it in a 12-week course for undergraduates and postgraduate law students at the School of Law at Queen's University in Belfast.[48] The first iteration of the second case study started in 2019 and was conducted at the Osaka University of Economics and Law with third-year undergraduate students. The second case study used the "Laws of War" downloadable content module.[49]

Queen's University School of Law

In the first case study, the instructors created five interactive scenarios for the course, covering distinction, proportionality, humanitarian access for the ICRC, war crimes, and the specific obligations of special forces units. The scenarios were then proofed by a group of postgraduate students who had different levels of IHL knowledge and who were given a multiple choice test after running through the scenarios. After incorporating the test group's feedback into the curriculum and the scenarios, the scenarios were then used with about 40 students in an IHL course. The results of their scenario work were then assessed by a multiple-choice test, which was to comprise 20 percent of their course grade.[50]

The instructors found that creating the interactive scenarios and then running them for many students at the same time on the hardware they had purchased for the course was both time-consuming and technologically complex. These factors degraded the students' game experience to a significant extent and, in some cases, resulted in negative impacts to their test scores. Further, although the students found the scenario work interesting, for many it was a new experience to have their academic performance assessed in this way. Finally, in evaluating the results of the scenario-based instruction, one thing that appears to have surprised the instructors was the number of students who chose options in the scenario play that resulted in IHL violations. The instructors realized, however, that the format of the assessment did not allow for the students to explain why they chose the wrong solution.[51]

On these bases, the instructors decided to not include the students' marks on the scenarios test in their final grades. The instructors concluded that it would have been better to use the interactive scenarios as a formative assessment instead of a summative one.[52] In subsequent iterations, the students worked with the scenarios in small groups, rather than as individuals, which the instructors found bolstered the students' critical thinking and problem-solving skills related to IHL.[53]

Osaka University of Economics and Law

The second case study, from 2020, was based on the experiences of 14 third-year undergraduate students in playing the simulation in the "Laws of War" downloadable content module that included civilians and those no longer in combat. Most of the students had already taken some courses associated with international law, and half had taken courses that included instruction on IHL.[54] Before they played the simulation, the students were directed to first view a lecture on IHL that dealt with the core principles of protection of civilians, such as only attacking military targets and not attacking civilians, and the need to limit collateral damage to civilians and private property.[55] After the students played the simulation, the instructor conducted semi-structured interviews with them and analyzed the automated record of their simulation play.[56]

The instructor found that all the students exhibited one of six patterns of learning in playing the simulation.[57] Some students exhibited a pattern the researcher termed as "Smooth IHL Learning with the Use of Knowledge Already Acquired," which was associated with high attendance rates in classes related to IHL and relatively good grades and was marked by a high level of attention to the introductory lecture. These students easily learned to apply the IHL principles being taught and developed a "comparatively high degree" of "imagining real fighting conditions and feeling empathy for real combatants."[58]

Conversely, other students exhibited a learning pattern the researcher termed "Disregarding the Instructor's Lectures and Committing Illegal Acts." This pattern was characterized by not paying much attention to the introductory lecture and instead learning the norms through admonitions given during the game as a result of committing illegal acts against those not in combat and damaging private property. This led to an incomplete learning of IHL by the students, because they were not able to engage with the larger picture of IHL requirements, and instead they learned only to not commit certain acts.[59] As a result, for example, they were not able to adequately identify the proper targets of attack under IHL in other situations.[60] Interestingly, in two subsequent iterations of game play, the researcher found that the students all continued to fall into one of the six learning patterns he identified in the first test.[61]

The instructor also found that whether the students paid attention to the introductory lecture was the single most important factor in learning the IHL concepts addressed in the simulation. In fact, students who had no prior academic IHL experience but who paid attention to the lecture achieved the same level of learning as those who already had some experience.[62] Further, developing empathy for the combatants and being able to imagine the conditions in which they were fighting was associated with positive IHL learning outcomes in playing the game.[63]

Finally, the students who learned through paying attention to the game's admonitions after committing violations largely achieved the same level of learning about the specific applications of IHL as if they had paid attention to the introductory lecture. In the interviews the instructor conducted after the students played the game, he did not ask them directly why they had not acted in compliance with IHL when they made their decisions whether to shoot. The students who showed this playing style, however, did tend to have relatively rich experiences already in playing similar first-person shooter war video games.[64] The instructor concluded that to ensure that the desired learning of IHL principles occurred, it was necessary to build redundancy into the curriculum by using both the lecture for students who were more process-oriented and the admonitions during the game for those who preferred to learn the hard way.[65] It is also worth noting the similarity between the moral decision reasoning methodology used by these students and that used by the sleep-deprived Norwegian cadets in the first case study—essentially a rules-based approach.

The instructor also identified something very important that potentially militates against tailoring IHL learning too closely to cultural or national experiences, or what may, in fact, be distorted politicized perspectives of those experiences. For example, a student in one of the game iterations was from China, and after playing the "Laws of War" module, the student recognized that there was a difference between the ways IHL had been presented back home in China as compared to its presentation in the module.[66] The instructor noted that on this basis, "What should be avoided at all costs is unfair justification for inappropriate conduct on the basis of biased interpretation of IHL rules."[67]

Both studies suggest that war video games, properly constructed and carefully employed, can be a useful and engaging way to instruct on basic IHL principles. The study with the students in Northern Ireland shows that students' motivations in playing the game can impact the results of the assessments the instructors are seeking to generate. The study involving the students in Japan suggests that instruction, and by extension the instructor, is still important in effectively teaching IHL when using war video games. For those who wish to learn the rules through trial-and-error-without-consequence, however, irrespective of whether it is an established pattern for them because of their previous game play, or it is just a demonstration of their preferred learning style in general, the role of the virtual IHL admonisher in the game becomes less coach and more cop. This potentially presents challenges in casting trainer avatars who can be credible and effective in both virtual roles.

From an ethical perspective, and probably from political and legal ones as well, it is not clear that everyone would be comfortable with troops learning to properly protect real civilians and detainees through recklessly endangering their virtual representations.[68] Steps could be taken to mitigate this, however. For example, the video war game could be programmed to identify troops that used the trial-and-error learning style without the benefit of initial virtual IHL instruction. Although soldiers who used this learning style might achieve a passing grade on the virtual training (even if they incurred a point penalty for errors in applying IHL), they would also have identified themselves as needing additional training, and perhaps mentoring.

So that it was not viewed as punishment, any additional IHL session would likely need to be done in a way that they would find professionally rewarding, such as in a discussion or seminar format with credible instructors. Another possibility would be requiring them to train with the war video games in teams, with people whom they worked with and depended upon in the geophysical world. This way, their individual styles of play would no longer be without real-world consequences to them, particularly if there were a shared reward for the team score in the game with the highest rate of IHL compliance.

Analysis

Resiliency in moral reasoning

The Norwegian study on the degradation of moral decision-making skills did not specifically relate to IHL, but it is pertinent nonetheless to the effectiveness of IHL training. Different writers have emphatically addressed the need to foster resiliency in the ethical decision-making of soldiers and to do so through realistic training.[69] What does not appear to have been substantively addressed in the literature, however, is what this resiliency should look like, or how it could be planned for.

The results of the experiment with the Australian officers and NCOs described in Chapter 2, in which the participants deciding whether to conduct an attack were given different scenarios as to peer and legal assessments of the attack's propriety, suggest that the officers were applying the principled moral reasoning tested in the Norwegian experiment. The results could also be interpreted as showing that the NCOs were not, and they were instead generally taking a more rules-based approach. Jenks has suggested that reliance on simplified rules for IHL training beyond that given to soldiers in basic training is not helpful. As he notes, "part of the underlying training challenge is that much of IHL is predicated on the contextual reasonableness of decisions made under stressful circumstances and with incomplete information."[70]

Jenks is not wrong. This does not mean, however, that the Australian NCOs' reasoning in the experiment necessarily resulted in choices inconsistent with IHL. If they were accustomed to taking a more rules-based approach, say, one consistent with the 10 Soldier's Rules used in US Army training, their decisions would likely still be generally compliant with IHL in stressful situations. The lead researcher in the Norwegian study has observed, "The ethical challenge is therefore to have a well-adapted and developed moral rules-set—that is also understood by the crews. You will probably get what you have in the rules."[71]

Perhaps ethical resiliency in the IHL education and training context means developing layers of reasoning methodologies in soldiers. This approach would recognize that the stresses of combat might temporarily depress more complex reasoning skills, but that an irreducible core of compliant reasoning can be developed and sustained even under very challenging conditions. This casts tools such as the 10 Soldier's Rules in a more favorable light—these are not just simplifications of IHL that can be easily memorized, they also can be taught and trained as the basic part of a reasoning system methodology to which exhausted and worried minds could default when necessary and still do things mostly right.

Realism and risk in developing IHL decision-making skills

In contrast to the Norwegian study that documented the negative effects of stressors like those experienced in combat on the use of high-level moral reasoning, the Swiss study focused on the development of those skills and their duration under more ordinary conditions. The Swiss experiment is very useful because it suggests that as with the moral dilemmas used in the Norwegian study, to increase the effectiveness of the IHL education and training troops will apply in the field in ethically challenging situations, the examples that are used likely need to be stressful in their own right—they need to pose the risk of significant harm if not resolved properly and they need to be realistic.

There is a caveat to this approach—the better the example of a real-world dilemma under these criteria, the more likely it is to cast an unfavorable light on at least some of the actors involved. If the examples are coming from one's own country's military's experiences, it could be politically challenging to implement in an education and training program. Further, perhaps echoing Talbert and Wolfendale's suggestion that IHL education include instruction on causes of war crimes and examples from one's own military service and country to be effective,[72] the Brereton Report recommended this approach for the Australian special forces.[73] At the time of this writing, however, it does not appear that any criminal proceedings involving Australian special forces have been completed, and given the manner in which the Brereton Report investigation had to be conducted, it is not clear that all or even the most important alleged cases of war crimes would actually result in criminal convictions.[74] Acquittals at courts-martial make for only modestly useful IHL training case studies.

Finally, the Swiss study indicates that IHL training cannot just be considered another block of military training. The reasoning skills needed to properly apply IHL in complex situations are not necessarily those used to solve other military problems, even by otherwise well-trained and educated troops. Given this, it is important to be mindful of the personal and professional development that students will have experienced before receiving IHL education and training. Potentially, putting national differences aside, there is likely a significant difference from a teaching perspective between professional audiences that are 28 years old as with the Swiss officers versus approximately 36 years old as with the US officers at CGSC.

Austere conditions do not preclude careful crafting and data collection

The case study from Mali shows that even in austere training environments with challenging training audiences, intensive preparation to understand the psychosocial context in which the soldiers are operating and the nature of the actual IHL compliance issues that have been observed in the areas to which they will deploy can serve to mitigate the impacts of these obstacles to learning. Soldiers likely sense when the instruction given to them has been thoughtfully tailored to their situations, and this likely impacts the credibility of the instructors in a positive way.

Consistent with the preference expressed by the Filipino soldiers in the "Roots of Restraint" study, civilian IHL instructors can be very credible with troops. In the Mali case study, the lead civilian instructor lodged in the barracks at the training site and was with each battalion for the full 10 weeks of instruction. Further, she did not restrict her work to the classroom; instead, she was also present and observing the soldiers as they went through their tactical exercises, and she assisted the tactical military instructors in learning what they should look for in the soldiers' handling of the IHL-related themes embedded in the exercises.[75]

In addition, even in the most basic of training curricula, there are ways to tie IHL compliance to positive military values such as professionalism that will register with a training audience. Finally, useful empirical assessment is not something that can only be conducted under laboratory conditions. Data relevant to IHL training effectiveness can also be gathered under field conditions, and prior planning that makes collection part of even a lean training curriculum from the beginning probably has a significant impact on collection and analysis.

Leader development, emotional stress, and nationality of case studies

Because of the lack of a pretraining survey before the beginning of the US Army battalion's leadership development program, among other limitations with the data collection and the self-selecting nature of the survey respondents, a degree of caution is necessary in distilling lessons learned from that case study. The survey results, however, are consistent with the ICRC's "Roots of Restraint" assessment of IHL training effectiveness and the battlefield ethics training program in Iraq in important ways. It matters what leaders think about IHL and how they express this to their subordinates.

Taking a multidisciplinary approach to IHL training, and linking it to values and ethical decision-making, and to experiences, appears to register with many training audiences irrespective of their ranks. It also appears possible to develop a sense of emotional stress that makes the training more memorable through an intensive visitation of historical sites associated with IHL and human rights atrocities without needing to subject training audiences to actual physical stresses such as hunger or fatigue. Memorable IHL training need not be physically painful to register with students and to become something they incorporate into either their individual codes of conduct or their sense of a shared positive professional identity.

Further, the US leadership development program participants found the case study of the three different German company commanders to be largely effective in understanding the challenging circumstances those commanders found themselves in regarding their choices in responding to the battalion commander's illegal order. Although using war crime examples from one's own service and country in IHL education certainly has value from the perspective of making soldiers realize that they too could become perpetrators,[76] these examples might be better suited to developing a historical appreciation of this reality rather than developing the moral decision-making skills necessary to keep it from happening. Instead of identical nationality, what is instead likely more useful are case studies with well-documented factual bases and examples of different decision-making processes being used by different commanders in similarly situated units to reach different conclusions, such as the "Ordinary Soldiers" lesson plan used by the battalion.

Rewards and challenges posed by the use of war video games

The ICRC's efforts to engage militaries in the use of visual simulations for education and training and the video game industry to include IHL content in war video games show great promise. These data-driven domains likely lend themselves to the collection of assessment data that could be analyzed remotely and quickly through automation. The case studies from Northern Ireland and Japan show that young students favor the use of these tools and that there are certain advantages that this type of IHL training can offer.

At the same time, the use of these games is not without its challenges in terms of ensuring ethical behaviors are learned in ethical ways. This is an area that deserves significant research because these concerns are not fanciful. Even if in the end researchers conclude that war video game players clearly recognize that a game is just a game, the issue identified in the case study from Japan remains—players who learn to apply IHL principles only by mistake might not develop an understanding of IHL sufficient to allow them to effectively apply it in situations different from the specific ones in the game in which they harmed civilians and detainees.

A further issue with this sort of training is figuring out where to include the role of military leader, whether officer or NCO, how that person is best represented in the game, and what functionality is associated with them in the game. For example, it could be worthwhile to explore how war video game avatars could become inspiring in terms of professional values associated with IHL compliance, rather than just agents of admonishment and enforcement when the players make errors. In the long run, this could be more useful than just being a source of virtual discipline in the event of hypothetical misbehavior.

Summary

Taken together, these case studies provide creative and practical examples of the work different instructors and researchers have done to build an assessment of training effectiveness into their instructional designs, in very different teaching and training situations. The Norwegian and Swiss studies provide useful information regarding the resilience and the duration of more highly developed moral reasoning skills. Developing these skills requires focused instruction, and they can endure for decent periods of time, but they are a subject to sharp degradation under conditions of stress, like those found in combat. But these skills also appear to be resilient and apparently rebound when the stressors are relieved, such as by getting some sleep.

The training of the new Malian soldiers shows two important points. First, careful and holistic tailoring of an IHL training program to the needs of the training audience, both cognitive and emotional, does not require a lot of money, and it can be very effective. Second, austere training environments are no excuse for not devising creative ways to collect data and import empirical assessment into an IHL training program.

Unlike the Malian soldiers, the soldiers from the US Army battalion in Germany were not preparing for imminent combat deployment. In this sense, the battalion's leadership development program lacked the stress of the operational intensity of the Malian soldiers' IHL training. Importantly though, the moral intensity of the training can generate its own level of emotional stress to make the training more memorable, as the battalion did with its staff ride to Auschwitz and to Nuremberg.

The two case studies involving the use of war video games of university students are also important contributions to the field of empirical assessment of IHL instruction. The use of electronic simulations and games in soldiers' training is very likely to increase in the future, both because of cost considerations and because of customer demand among younger, technologically savvy soldiers. However, there are many issues that need to be addressed regarding the use of these platforms for IHL education and training from ethical and practical perspectives prior to launching on their large-scale use.

Perhaps the steps these researchers, educators, and officers have taken to include assessment and how to conduct it represent starting points for the development of best practices in the use of empirical assessment of IHL education and training efficacy. Even an imperfect generation of quantitative and qualitative data on how the IHL training was received and whether it had any enduring impacts can provide an objective basis for a systematic approach to designing IHL education and training curricula, and for making improvements to methodologies for measuring any changes in attitudes and behaviors regarding IHL brought about by this instruction.

You have stayed with me as we waded through data and statistical analyses related to IHL education and training, and details on curriculum design and methods of delivery. I hope you have found these different case studies interesting and useful in terms of prompting your own thoughts on how we might make IHL training more effective. At the beginning of this book,

I informed you I had changed my mind about the wisdom of focusing almost exclusively on the legal norms of IHL in making IHL training more effective, but I did not explain why. After having read through the case studies, you likely have a good idea at this point of some of the things that have influenced me in changing my approach, but I now owe you a fuller explanation. Further, having patiently listened to my arguments for taking a different approach to IHL education and training, I also owe you an assessment of the challenges in implementing it.

CONCLUSION

Even as modern warfare evolves to become more automated in many respects, such as using drones and crewless warships,[1] it is also bumping up against the reality of "war amongst the people." As General Sir Rupert Smith describes in his influential work *The Utility of Force*, trends such as increasing global populations, greater urbanization, and resource scarcity mean that in many operations the key terrain is not actually land at all, but instead the perceptions, attitudes, and behaviors of the people who live there.[2] Information technology is likely accelerating this trend. For example, as shown by the investigations of the insurrection by supporters of President Trump against the legislative branch of the US government in early 2021,[3] social media has become crucially important in mobilizing widely distributed groups of people and individuals to quickly take coordinated actions they would not otherwise be able to easily do.

Whether armed forces fighting in the people's presence comply with IHL is likely of grave importance to them and their families, and this will matter to them in deciding whom they want to support. Distinguished writers have argued that one method to increase troops' compliance with IHL is to provide them training that helps them better understand the culture of the people among whom they might be fighting.[4] There are documented instances of this proving useful, for example, the cultural lesson learned by one company of US Marines garrisoning the Fallujah Peninsula on the Euphrates River in Iraq in 2007. The economy of the area was based on agriculture, and this required pumping water from the river into crop fields. Unfortunately, the flooded fields made it difficult to patrol the area, so the Marines had persuaded farmers to not use the pumping stations.[5]

As the economy suffered, local Iraqis began emplacing improvised explosive devices along the routes traveled by the Marines. After negotiations, the Marines realized how their actions were triggering potentially lethal acts against them, and so the pumping stations were turned back on.[6] Suppose, however, the Marines had ignored the economic impacts of their actions, and eventually improvised explosive devices began claiming Marine casualties.

This intense combat exposure might then have become a factor in changing the Marines' attitudes and behaviors toward the local civilians, potentially at some point resulting in feelings of rage overcoming ordinary discipline and a professional ethos regarding treatment of civilians.

There are concerns, however, just how effective cultural training is. For example, several years before the Brereton Report was published, a researcher working with Australian special forces conducted a survey to determine the troops' true feelings regarding Islam. One hundred and eighty-two troops from four different special forces units participated, 80 percent of whom had received cultural training to allow them to interact more smoothly and respectfully with civilians in Islamic countries. Ninety-one percent of those who had received this training agreed with the statement, "The Muslim religion promotes violence and terrorism."[7] This suggests that the impact of cultural knowledge training is perhaps too uneven to be relied upon heavily in keeping troops compliant with IHL.

As to the need for effective IHL education and training, the potential cost of IHL violations is very high, both in terms of injuring individuals' health, rights, and dignity, on one hand, and compromising mission success, on the other. Although IHL instruction is required by international law, and it is undoubtedly a very positive thing for military forces to educate and train their personnel in IHL using qualified instructors with quality instructional materials, well-delivered training by itself is not enough to ensure that the training is effective in the field. When IHL training fails, and civilians and detainees are hurt or killed, traditional legal approaches and processes often fail to provide meaningful outcomes for those who suffered. In many cases, the damages are too severe; in the event of deaths, the results are irreparable. Further, it is difficult to demonstrate that prosecutions before international tribunals are effective in preventing violations of IHL through deterrence.

Morally and ethically, as well as from a practical perspective, steps that could be taken to improve IHL compliance and prevent violations are worthwhile investments in international and human security. What I propose is neither a substitute for academic classes that allow students to engage deeply with IHL and develop their understanding of its scope and complexity, nor for realistic and gritty STX scenarios with highly trained role players that test soldiers' application of IHL in an environment much closer to that found in the field in operations. It is instead a multidisciplinary system that requires all of these, driven by data, focused on fostering IHL values as part of each soldier's personal and professional identity, and led by leaders. Before I set out the specific features I think this sort of education and training should have and the challenges that implementing it would likely face, I need to first explain how I came to believe that IHL training that focuses essentially only on the legal norms is not effective.

Change Does Not Come Easy

My thinking about the effectiveness of IHL training began to change in 2011 as I was retiring from the Army. By chance, I attended a workshop at the US Holocaust Memorial Museum on including more information about the Holocaust and genocide in general in military education. Dr. Waitman Beorn, a former US Army cavalry officer, presented us with material from his new book, *Marching into Darkness: The Wehrmacht and the Holocaust in Belarus*, about a particular German reserve infantry battalion pulling rear area security duty in eastern Belarus in 1941. His research was the impetus for the "Ordinary Soldiers" case study mentioned in the previous chapter, used by the US Army battalion in Germany.

One day in early October 1941, the battalion commander ordered each of his maneuver company commanders to kill all the Jewish civilians in their respective areas of operation, on the pretext that the Jews were supporting partisan fighters. One company commander, who was a member of the Nazi SS in civilian life, who had been a Nazi Party member since 1929, and who was known by his troops to be "antireligious," complied immediately. A second company commander, a schoolteacher when not in uniform and a 47-year-old World War I veteran, considered the order and then rejected it, informing the battalion commander that he was not going to have his soldiers get their hands dirty with such things. The third company commander at first sought to avoid carrying out the executions, but once the battalion commander confirmed the order in writing, he asked his headquarters staff for volunteers to kill the Jews. No one stepped forward, so he ordered the company's first sergeant to see to the executions, while he himself then took care of some administrative tasks.[8]

Remember, although reprisals against civilians for support to irregular combatants did not become illegal until the 1949 Geneva Conventions,[9] reprisals still had to be proportional in forcing civilians to cease their support.[10] As the German courts that tried the third company commander and the company's first sergeant after World War II concluded, this could include executing those civilians who actually provided the support or even a segment of a population that was innocent.[11] Killing entire populations, however, was disproportionate.

So, a single illegal order, given in the clear. Three different responses from three small unit commanders who were essentially equals in rank and responsibilities, and whose operational experiences, at least in terms of this world war, had been nearly identical and not particularly noteworthy. Further, like the second company commander, the third company commander (the one who initially hesitated to comply with the order) was also a World War I veteran and a schoolteacher in civilian life. In light of their strong similarities, what accounted for these two men's very different approaches to complying with IHL as it existed at that time?

Dr. Beorn corresponded with surviving family members of the commander who refused and learned that, although he was a Nazi Party member, as all civil servants such as teachers had to be to hold their positions, he was not particularly enthused with Nazi principles. He also had discouraged his son from joining the Hitler Youth. Further, his family remembered him as a very religious man.[12] Importantly, his refusal of the order was not based on its illegality—instead, he rejected it as being contrary to his sense of the honorable professionalism of his troops.

Clearly, there was much more at play here than the law in the moral and ethical decision-making of these officers related to applying IHL. Intrigued, I joined Dr. Beorn and other Holocaust historians and educators in putting together a lesson plan based on the case study. In our research, we also learned about the work of Dr. Felix Römer and his team in researching the recordings made by US Army Military Intelligence of conversations between different Wehrmacht prisoners of war at Fort Hunt, Virginia, as they awaited transportation to their eventual camps in the interior United States. For many of these German soldiers, peer pressure and senses of unit loyalty were reasons for engaging in atrocities against those who were not in combat—but importantly, they were also the reasons given for not doing so. Soldiers who did not engage in atrocities criticized those who had, and those who had often justified their actions based on the threat posed to them and their units.[13]

Like my teammates, I have used the lesson plan with many different audiences, US civilian and military and international military officers, over the last several years. The version of the lesson plan I generally use requires the training audience to discuss tasks that I give them in small groups, and they then brief their solutions back to the whole class. As a result of this feedback in class, I have learned two important things that have changed the way I view IHL education and training.

First, no military value, however deeply cherished, is an absolute good. Military organizations such as the US Army invest a great deal of effort into establishing the positive values that officers and soldiers are expected to incorporate into their work and even into their lives as military professionals. Unfortunately, I see now that not enough time is spent helping soldiers develop the decision-making skills that would allow them to weigh and resolve what might appear to be conflicts between equally positive values. The different decisions of the two German company commanders who were both World

War I veterans highlight this. For one, the loyalty to his troops appears to have won out; for the other, perhaps his primary value was loyalty to his chain of command. Spending time figuring out why they came to these different conclusions is a useful way to begin considering the borders of our own ethical decision-making processes.

Second, effective training in IHL needs to be keyed to the cultural, social, and ethical norms of restraint that members of training audiences will have as individuals, in addition to any positive norms of professional restraint they develop that are consistent with IHL. In 2018, I had the opportunity to work with a large group of Mexican naval officers, both line and legal advisors, using the lesson plan. This was the first time I used the lesson plan with a group of students who were all from the same country other than the United States. The task for their small group work was to develop a course of action sketch for the development of a new military education curriculum to be used with Mexican officers to prevent illegal acts against those who were not in combat.

As part of their sketches, the small groups had to state the values that they would emphasize in the instruction to help convince the students to comply with IHL. Two of the small groups specifically identified the upholding of family honor as an important value in fostering compliance, and the others concurred. In the times I had taught the lesson plan before with international students, family honor had not been part of any small group's solution. Never before, though, did I have a group of students where cultural values such as this would not be diluted by the purposeful mixing I had done of their small groups by nationality before they began. My desire for consensus responses across groups with mixed nationalities—a purposeful lesson design feature, an assumedly positive thing—meant that I had missed important data related to IHL compliance. Important data that was not legal in nature, but quite significant.

Consistent with the "Roots of Restraint in War" study, I now accept that effective IHL training needs to be tailored to different training audiences and that it must resonate with them on an emotional level as well as a cognitive level. Good leaders find ways to address both. I am still struck by the remarkable improvements in combat soldiers' attitudes and behaviors regarding IHL shown by the battlefield ethics training program in Iraq, and so I also understand that there is no substitute for empirical data in assessing whether training has had its intended effects. Mindful of this, I now turn to what I believe should be the features of an effective IHL training program that is affordable, practicable, led by leaders, supported by multidisciplinary specialists, oriented on positive shared military values, and, importantly, driven by data.

The Components of a Path Forward, and the Challenges

Who are they? How do they change?

To create a more effective IHL training program from the beginning, we should first start with an assessment of troops when they enter basic training. This would set a useful benchmark to document their attitudes and perceptions regarding the ways civilians and detainees should be treated. Some might argue that this is not necessary, because the basic training itself will instill the desired values and traits expected of newly trained young soldiers—irrespective of the values and traits they brought with them into the military. Until it is tested, however, this position is supposition. Comparing that initial data with survey results generated upon their completion of basic training would allow us to tease out the impacts of their initial military socialization on these topics.

For both enlisted soldiers and officers, we should gather this data every time they participate in a formal military education and training program,[14] other than those that are of short duration and which are specifically geared toward acquiring technical skills. To provide opportunities to properly reinforce the internalization of the values necessary for them to understand and comply with IHL, formal education and training programs should include instruction that links leadership, IHL, and ethical decision-making. Consistent with the views of the young majors at CGSC in 2001 on the most effective forms of IHL training, the data collected might be most useful if it is generated during instruction that models the discussions and seminar-style training on these issues that we would want these leaders to be able to competently conduct with their subordinates back at their units.

Further, as the Swiss case study suggests, the skills needed to make a sound ethical decision in a complex situation may need to be specifically trained—even officers experienced in regular military problem solving struggled at first to do it effectively in that study. For example, merely providing information such as the US Army's 10 Soldier's Rules and the official US Army values to new soldiers does not provide a methodological bridge between these two sets of abstract things to help them sort out conflicts between positive values of apparently equal weight in real life. If data were collected only on the new soldiers' ability to list these rules or values, it might show some level of familiarity with the terms, but it would not provide information on whether they could apply them effectively.

However, as shown by the Norwegian case study with sleep-deprived cadets, a set of rules such as this might, in fact, be the base level of a resilient moral reasoning system we would want every officer and soldier to internalize. Testing whether the instruction has been effective in accomplishing this might require more involved assessments conducted under conditions of stress. A point raised by the survey of the majors at Fort Leavenworth could provide a buttress for such a default setting. Several survey respondents identified the need to find a more tangible reason for soldiers to follow IHL than the possibility that their adversaries might reciprocate. If IHL principles become internalized as part of a professional military ethos, then the grounding for IHL compliance becomes much more basic, perhaps even existential to a degree—"We do not follow IHL because of how the enemy might behave, we follow IHL because it is part of who we are."

Leaving aside for the moment the logistical challenges posed by the data collection, analysis, and storage that would be necessary to create and use this knowledge base of our troops, the development of it would necessitate changes in the ways militaries conduct IHL education and training—ways in which they are currently invested. To generate the data that would be most useful, the education and training curricula would need to begin changing to accommodate instruction that takes a multidisciplinary approach and focuses on leadership, moral reasoning, and professional military values. However, this need not happen all at once. Pilot programs that can run in parallel with existing courses using selected groups of students or trainees could provide a sufficient sample to harvest the data on soldiers' perceptions, attitudes, and behaviors, and that information could guide change in the larger IHL education and training system.

Internalizing IHL principles as part of an honorable professionalism

Changing long-standing perceptions, attitudes, and behaviors is not easy. Finding ways to promote soldiers internalizing IHL principles voluntarily and fitting them into their individual systems of beliefs and values so that they will act quickly and competently upon them in challenging situations is likely to be an inexact science. Working with this reality is probably easier in a military setting where the professional ethic that all members are expected to share can be clearly defined and reinforced by education, training, and conduct in actual operations. However, this challenge is not likely to disappear completely—this is just a reflection of human nature.

One possible way forward is to find a driver of the shared professional ethic, in both its formal and informal aspects, and to leverage that force to promote the uptake and assimilation of IHL principles. In his study of the opposing sides in Uganda's civil war in the 1980s, Bell makes a persuasive case for the military culture of the National Resistance Army (NRA) and its pervasive organizational norm of civilian protection being primarily responsible for the low numbers of civilian deaths attributed to it. Bell identified four factors that fostered the norm's internalization across the NRA: the consistent promotion of the norm by NRA leaders at all levels, the intensive political indoctrination that all NRA soldiers received in the norm as part of its values-based approach to armed conflict, strict discipline for violators of the norms, and interestingly, informal socialization measures that promoted internalization of the norm within NRA soldiers.[15]

These informal measures included unit self-critique sessions, the development of close bonds between the soldiers, and the notion of " 'conscious discipline,' principles that prioritized discipline through the internalization of organizational norms rather than through rules and punishment."[16] The NRA's Marxist and Maoist ideological orientation that undergirded these measures would not likely translate well to militaries of liberal democracies, but there might be useful analogs. For example, in the US Army, a promising candidate is an individual soldier's fear of being seen by comrades as undependable or selfish because he or she does not personally take the steps necessary to ensure that his or her conduct positively impacts the unit's performance and safety. This is what noted author and war correspondent Sebastian Junger has termed the "Zen of not fucking up."[17]

In his bestselling book *War*, Junger recounts his experiences with a platoon of US soldiers at a remote outpost in Afghanistan's Korengal Valley between 2007 and 2008. One time he attended a council meeting of Afghan elders wearing an old Army shirt, but he forgot to take it with him when he left. This was a significant problem, because the shirt could have been taken by one of the elders and given to an enemy fighter, who might then be able to disguise himself as a US soldier. Junger realized from the soldiers' reactions to his mistake that they were extremely disappointed in him, because his failure to be mindful in his own actions meant that he had risked the safety of the unit.[18]

The MHAT V surveys from Afghanistan and Iraq, detailed in Chapter 3, showed a very interesting relationship between two sets of responses by the combat soldier participants. The duty to report violations of IHL is a fundamental basis for compliance with this body of law, but only about a third of respondents said that they would report a comrade for verbal abuse of civilians, unnecessarily damaging private property, or physically striking an innocent civilian. Further, only slightly more than 40 percent said they would report a comrade for injuring or killing someone who was not in combat. At the same time, however, when the questions moved from the hypothetical to the real, only between 4 and 5 percent said that they had physically struck someone who was not in combat when it was not necessary.

This suggests two things to me. First, the bonds between soldiers can be very strong, strong enough to keep them from taking the affirmative step of reporting others for even very serious violations, although mediated to a degree by the seriousness of the offense. This strength must be recognized as having positive aspects as well, and these must be used to advantage. For example, a study of 20 British Royal Air Force bomb disposal officers revealed that despite their dangerous jobs, the relationship between the stress they felt and their identification as a rather unique work group "was mediated by perceptions of social support provided specifically by in-group members." In other words, their group identity was "a basis for receiving and benefitting from the support of fellow group members—support which in turn can serve as a buffer against the adverse effects of stress."[19] So, the bonds between comrades that might lead to one not reporting another for an IHL violation could, at the same time, help protect soldiers from combat stress and boost their mental health, which could have a positive effect on compliance with IHL.

Second, the latitude in behavior that these US soldiers in Afghanistan and Iraq were apparently willing to tolerate in their comrades was not matched by the self-discipline they used to keep themselves in check. This strength too must be recognized, for it indicates an existing reservoir of positive individual and professional identity consistent with IHL compliance that can be tapped to increase internalization of IHL principles.

From the perspective of Junger's salty zen, if compliance with IHL in all respects could be translated in carefully constructed education and training curricula to become part of the shared ethic of military professionalism, individual soldiers could be more likely to see any failure to follow IHL not as a matter of personal choice by their peers. Instead, violating IHL would be viewed as an expression of selfishness, perhaps even evidence of cowardice, and unprofessionally not meeting the standards that keep everyone as safe as possible and help them all get back home when their deployment is done. Peer pressure then becomes a positive thing, allowing soldiers to be comfortable in confronting comrades who might be starting to go astray, because they know the judgment of the group is behind them.

There is an important caveat to being successful in taking this kind of approach. If soldiers were to effectively internalize IHL principles in this manner, and act upon them professionally in taking positive steps in their work and actions, but the chain of command and the rest of the organization do not fully back them and support them, the negative psychological impact on the soldiers could be very pronounced.

In the case of the US Army lieutenant who ordered his soldiers to kill two Afghan civilians that I noted earlier in Chapter 4, his soldiers reported him for murder. As the case went through the court-martial process, soldiers in this platoon had to deal with being thought of as a rogue unit by some, and as betrayers and cowards by others. After they returned to the United States, they received little official recognition for their positive actions in combat, and some began experiencing mental health issues and substance abuse. Soldiers began to have discipline problems, and a number left the Army. Some started taking extraordinarily dangerous risks. One later committed suicide; others tried to. As one of the former soldiers explained,

> I thought of the Army as this altruistic thing. I thought it was perfect and honorable. It pains me to tell you how stupid and naïve I was. The [lieutenant's crimes] just broke my faith. [...] And once you lose your values and your faith, the Army is just another job you hate.[20]

The then president's pardon of the lieutenant accentuated the negative effects of the murders on several of the former platoon members.[21] The risk of effects like these will need to be reckoned with on the path to more effective IHL training. One possible way to mitigate this risk is through feedback. When soldiers do the right thing, they need to be supported by the command. When it is serious like this incident, leaders need to talk to other soldiers as well and explain what the facts are and why reporting violations is a positive thing. This, of course, would present its own challenges in implementation—leaders would likely need instruction in how to do this effectively, in conformance with domestic criminal and privacy laws and regulations. This is perhaps an area where public affairs officers and attorneys could collaborate in developing instructional curricula and delivering instruction, and it might be best suited for delivery at the command and staff college level.

The role of the leader and growing leaders as instructors

In all the IHL training that soldiers and officers receive, we should tie it back to leadership and the ethics of leadership, and we should develop NCOs and commanders to be able to consistently engage with their subordinates on these topics in depth. The MHAT surveys showed that quality leadership serves a protective function in enhancing troops' mental health. Research on sexual violence against civilians and detainees in armed conflict, for example, indicates that military leaders play a very important role in preventing or reducing their soldiers' commission of such crimes, a role often positively reinforced by an organizational ethos forbidding these offenses.[22] Perceptions as to whether leadership is good would likely be positively impacted by frank discussions between leaders and the led as to the challenges they all face in making sure they make the right decisions, and by leaders explaining the moral and ethical decision-making processes they are modeling for their subordinates.

Perhaps most importantly, these discussions would provide a means to provide feedback, both from leaders to subordinates as to what they see in terms of progress and potential problem areas with IHL compliance, and from subordinates to leaders regarding what training is seen as being useful and what areas need to still be addressed. This might require some adjustments in attitude depending on military culture, because it has not been my experience that all leaders in different militaries are comfortable with this sort of information flow.

To some, implementing such a leader-led development program might seem daunting from a resources perspective. Commanders and NCOs are already too busy with the daily work of running units and watching over soldiers, so there would likely be well-founded concerns that this kind of program would be too expensive in terms of available time and the resources to deliver it. The battlefield ethics training in Iraq, the training of the new soldiers in Mali, and the work by the US Army battalion in Germany suggest, however, that it can be done sensibly and affordably—if the traditional training patterns are broken.

Insisting on the development of a lean curriculum, one that is essentially plug-and-play because leaders are modeling for their subordinates how to teach it as the subordinates are themselves being taught, would cut through a large amount of unnecessary training overhead. Focusing on the essential points rather than covering the vast area of IHL in the hopes of addressing everything is key, but not at the level of just providing a list of things to do and to not do. A focus like this is feasible when data collection and analysis is incorporated into the program from the beginning, to test whether the essential leadership, IHL, and ethics learning objectives are being met. Building such instruction and implementing it on a large scale poses resource challenges in terms of identifying personnel who have both the willingness to take a very different approach and the expertise to make it work. And it must work. There is likely limited tolerance in any military organization for experimentation that does not yield tangible results relatively quickly.

Multidisciplinary support to leaders

Once we have identified them, breaking professionals out of their occupational silos and making them work together in providing cohesive multidisciplinary support to leaders instructing on IHL presents organizational challenges, and challenges to the areas of responsibility of the organizations to which these professionals belong. These personnel are likely in high demand in their regular jobs already, and their parent organizations are unlikely to lend them out for long. Further, there will inevitably be questions as to who should be in charge because leadership will bear heavily on how issues regarding implementation are resolved. IHL itself is biased toward legal advisors assuming this role, but is this the most useful approach if we no longer believe that informing soldiers about the law is the best way to make them compliant with IHL?

We cannot lose sight of the fact that the mental health survey data from US combat troops in Afghanistan and Iraq shows that small unit personnel dynamics, command climate, frequency and intensity of combat encounters, sleep issues, and certain psychological problems that arise from combat deployments all have roles to play in whether combatants will comply with IHL. In addition, the survey results suggested that there was a linkage between the incidence of certain mental health problems and unethical behaviors on the battlefield, particularly soldiers' feelings of anger and rage. This knowledge could be very helpful to commanders in figuring out when their troops might need IHL refresher training. The expertise needed to make this information useful to the leaders who would now be shouldering the burden of IHL instruction is not generated in law schools, however.

Lawyers would of course continue to have an important role to play in the creation and delivery of this kind of program. However, the battlefield ethics training conducted in Iraq shows that there is a very real place for behavioral and mental health specialists, ethicists, and researchers with strong statistics and survey development skills in the creation of a lean and effective training program. The US Army battalion leadership development program in Germany likewise shows that there is useful space for counselors such as chaplains to assist in these efforts, as well as line officers.

Further, the training of new Malian soldiers by Beyond Peace shows that there is room for a holistic social and cultural assessment approach in developing and delivering an effective IHL training curriculum. It also confirms the findings of the "Roots of Restraint in War" study that the credibility of the instructor is in the eyes of the student, and that military instructors are not necessarily the most credible with different training audiences. In a similar vein, the case study of the moral decision-making course at the Swiss Military Academy shows that highly skilled civilian educators, psychologists, and individuals with human resource backgrounds can have an important role to play as well.

Leaders would need well-rounded teams to support them in the delivery of effective IHL training in the approach I am proposing, and the composition of these teams needs to reflect engagement with the social, educational, and cultural characteristics of the specific training audiences. This does not mean that this support is always physically present while the instruction is going on. Including these different experts from the beginning to create training programs would likely bring the value of their input to the assembly of an integrated product—without requiring them to actually be part of the delivery.

For this approach to work affordably, information technology will need to be leveraged.

As businesses, governments, and universities were forced to move many of their operations online because of the Covid-19 pandemic, internet platforms were developed that allowed effective remote collaboration on even very complex tasks. Further, information technology provides additional ways to be able to deliver specialist support remotely as needed, through services such as electronic help desks. Virtual multidisciplinary curriculum development teams, and online specialist support in curriculum delivery, could use digital infrastructure that has already been acquired by many organizations to deliver information and guidance to leaders without requiring new investments in central office space or work-related travel.

Embracing technology in instruction

Just as organizations quickly moved operations online during the pandemic because they had no real choice to do otherwise, different militaries had already begun experimenting with virtual reality in training important combat skills,[23] because their budgets and personnel training cycles were not seen as affording them much choice in the future either. We too must find ways to leverage virtual learning to achieve economy and effectiveness in the delivery of IHL training. The work of the ICRC with the war video game industry and the case studies of the university students in Northern Ireland and Japan show great promise in engaging not just civilian students but young soldiers as well. Further, for data to efficiently drive a lean set of education and training curricula, it is imperative to automate data collection and analysis about the training audience and their responses to the instruction. However, questions related to the proper content of IHL-related video games and how far we would be willing to go in allowing learning through the commission of virtual IHL violations against civilians and detainees will need to be addressed before the full potential of this type of training can be unlocked.

Thinking forward, these questions are also relevant in considering the need for effective IHL training for cyber commander and operators, which might be even more complex. It is one thing to take a first-person shooter war video game that uses realistic imagery and sounds and to figure out how to translate that into effective IHL training for troops to apply in the geophysical world. It is likely quite another to come up with war video games that realistically replicate a cyber conflict environment and allow cyber personnel to visualize what happens when action in cyberspace ripples into the geophysical world and impacts real people and things, as the Stuxnet computer virus appears to have done.[24]

An Estonian company, CybExer Technologies, has created cyber table-top exercises for European government bodies ranging from the European Defence Agency down to local municipalities.[25] One of the purposes of these exercises is to test the decision-making frameworks of the organizations and their members in handling cyber breaches.[26] Certain exercises include decision points that require the application of IHL.[27]

Interestingly, when exercise decision-makers are given the choice between using a cyber means to achieve an effect such as stopping the function of a utility that has both civilian and military uses, and using a kinetic means such as physical attack, they will often choose physical attack. This appears to be because they better understand the potential repercussions of actions conducted in the geophysical world—even though the cyber option might be less destructive.[28] The data generated from exercises like this could lead us into uncomfortable but necessary conversations about leadership, values, and ethics, and how these relate to IHL, especially when there are no perfect options and force must be used.

The development and maintenance of meaningful data

The battlefield ethics training in Iraq showed that it is possible to deliver effective leader-led IHL training in the middle of a combat deployment when it is guided by the collection and analysis of data relevant to what the troops are experiencing and how their experiences are impacting their attitudes and behaviors. To be meaningful from the perspective of effective IHL training, this means having the political and professional courage to ask troops uncomfortable questions about their views and behaviors regarding IHL related to civilians and detainees. Otherwise, it is not possible to know for certain the problem areas that need to be addressed, if any, nor whether the remedial measures put in place are having their intended effects. Fear of asking these questions because we are troubled by honest answers can only lead to mistreated civilians and detainees and a waste of resources.

Realistically, however, there could be well-founded concerns regarding the development and maintenance of this data, and whether its disclosure would expose civilian and military leaders to potential civil and criminal liability in legal processes. In terms of collecting data, the IHL training survey of new majors in the Class of 2002 at Fort Leavenworth had an opportunity to cross services and gather responses from both US Army and US Marine Corps officers. One challenge to overcome for any military service would be the extent to which it would be willing to share its data with other services and the degree to which it was willing to standardize the collection of information from its personnel with other services to make the data more easily comparable for analysis. Further, as the zero response rate by the US Army Special Forces students in the CGSC survey showed, there might be reluctance even within the same service to share information between different branches.

Taking a data-driven approach to IHL education and training, complemented by instruction by leaders who incorporate values in their lesson delivery, would fundamentally be an iterative process. The continuing collection of data and its continuing analysis, and the reciprocal feedback between the use of this analysis in the creation of curricula and the generation of data on the efficacy of the instruction, all suggest that this approach would be a long-term project that would require continued investment and a standing organization to run it. This raises important questions as to who should be tasked with sustaining the project, who gets to develop the courses of action that chart out its future development, and what influence they should have on the delivery of IHL education and training in real time.

There could also be credible concerns that honest data as to soldiers' attitudes toward IHL compliance could be used to embarrass governments and administrations politically. Military organizations might be concerned that the data could give legislators, and perhaps civil society organizations, a basis to insist on changes in IHL training that the military did not believe were warranted, useful, or affordable. Finally, the data might even be used by adversaries in information operations to disrupt relations between host nations and deploying forces, and potentially to encourage attacks on the militaries that collected it.

To mitigate these risks, it might be necessary to go beyond mere classification measures and depending on the nation that is collecting the data and analyzing it, to create domestic legislation that restricts not just the disclosure of the information but the possible uses that could be made of it in any legal proceedings. For example, in air safety investigations conducted of mishaps involving aircraft, to preserve US federal authorities' ability to gather information relevant to the accidents and to use the information to quickly recommend changes to improve public safety, much of the information developed during an investigation is inadmissible in any civil suit for damages in court.[29]

Further, the questions developed for use in the MHAT surveys appear to have been carefully crafted to avoid potential concerns of legal liability. For example, by using "ethical" to serve as a proxy for "legal," and by limiting the questions about individual soldier behaviors to certain acts that (although they were not strictly in compliance with IHL) also did not constitute grave breaches such as the murder of civilians or detainees, the MHAT surveys likely received more honest answers from the troops and defused legal concerns about the answers they gave. This is a sophisticated approach, but it could pose challenges to the organizations that would be tasked with maintaining the data: would they seek to limit the risks entailed by unauthorized disclosure of the data they held by sanitizing the data collected so that it was no longer potentially controversial, but consequently of limited operational value?

International and multinational IHL education and training

Taking the IHL education and training approach I am advocating must also include factoring in the roles of the ICRC and multinational collective defense organizations such as NATO. Regarding the ICRC, its willingness to embrace a shift in thinking on the part to be played by national, cultural, and military values, as well as its working with the war video game industry, suggests that it is positioned as an organization to assist countries with fewer resources in adopting such an approach. This could include collaboration in developing curricula tailored to particular regions in different languages, instruction in their use, and assistance in developing and maintaining the data necessary to make the approach work.

As to multinational operations, they have become a preferred means of conducting military missions for many countries for sound political, fiscal, and logistical reasons. Even though all countries have signed the Geneva Conventions, and a great many have signed Additional Protocol I, creating ROE for these missions that are uniformly understood when they involve the authority to use lethal force, which must of course be consistent with IHL, is no easy matter. Further, IHL training itself remains a national duty of the troop contributing nations,[30] so it is unlikely to be completely standardized across any multinational force.

NATO has attempted to harmonize national IHL training to the greatest extent practicable within the alliance. Its most recent version of IHL training doctrine takes an approach that largely reiterates IHL's principles and rules, and it provides basic guidance on tailoring training to different ranks and responsibilities, but it really goes no further. Nations are "encouraged" to evaluate their IHL training programs using a combination of different methods, including "classroom assessment, test papers and field training scenarios."[31] Although this is helpful, it is in certain important ways essentially business as usual in terms of IHL training, and it suggests that multinational implementation of the training approach I am advocating would face some inertia, if not resistance, in NATO and among the NATO troop contributing nations.

The bottom line

Despite these challenges, the data available to us now strongly argue for having leaders lead IHL training, expanding the teams that support leaders to include experts from different disciplines and perhaps from outside the military, emphasizing the role of values in the crucial decisions that troops make in combat, and designing IHL training from the beginning to have a data collection and analysis plan to ensure that more effective IHL training occurs. Case studies of different empirical approaches to IHL and IHL-related training suggest this approach can be affordable, sustainable, and measurable. The main question, though, is whether there would be sufficient national and international will and the associated resources to undertake this effort.

Irrespective of whether it is used in a national or an international setting, lawyers would still have important roles to play in the sort of approach I am advocating. But perhaps it is time for them to step back a bit so that we can find other ways that might more effectively advance IHL's goals of greater protection for civilians and detainees. This task will be complex, and it will require breaking no small number of existing education and training practice patterns. Resetting the legal advisors' role is among the first.

This task will also require resources, and acquiring them likely depends upon making the business case for spending money to reorient IHL education and training efforts. Only empirical assessment will secure a role for empirical assessment in achieving better protection for civilians and detainees in armed conflict. So, let us start by taking a simple first step; let us begin by first counting different things in the IHL education and training we currently provide and allow the analysis of this data to start our drive forward.

NOTES

Introduction

1   Charles S. Sullivan, "Game-Changing Strategies for Counterinsurgency and Complex Joint Operations," in *Airpower in Afghanistan 2005–10: The Air Commanders' Perspectives*, ed. Dag Hendriksen (Maxwell Air Force Base, AL: Air University Press, 2014), 162, 181–83, 203–6.

2   Evan J. Wallach, "Pray Fire First Gentlemen of France: Has 21st Century Chivalry Been Subsumed by Humanitarian Law?," *Harvard National Security Journal* 3 (2012): 432–33.

3   Altea Rossi, "Training Armed Forces in IHL: Just a Matter of Law?," OpinioJuris (blog), October 8, 2020, http://opiniojuris.org/2020/10/08/training-armed-forces-in-ihl-just-a-matter-of-law/.

4   William L. Shirer, *The Rise and Fall of the Third Reich: A History of Nazi Germany* (New York: Simon and Schuster, 1960), 952.

5   World Population Review, "World War Two Casualties by Country 2020," https://worldpopulationreview.com/country-rankings/world-war-two-casualties-by-country (accessed September 26, 2020).

6   ICRC, "The 1977 Additional Protocols to Geneva Conventions: A Historical Perspective," August 22, 1977, https://www.icrc.org/en/document/china-Yves-Sandoz-additional-protocols-40-years.

7   John F. Murphy, "Will-o'-the-Wisp? The Search for Law in Non-International Armed Conflicts," *International Legal Studies* 88 (2012): 15–16.

8   Bethany Lacina and Nils Peter Gleditsch, "Monitoring Trends in Global Combat: A New Dataset of Battle Deaths," *European Journal of Population* 21 (2005): 154–57, 159.

9   ICRC, "The 1977 Additional Protocols to Geneva Conventions."

10   See Theodore T. Richard, *Unofficial United States Guide to the First Additional Protocol to the Geneva Conventions of 12 August 1949* (Maxwell Air Force Base, AL: Air University Press, 2019).

11   Geneva Convention for the Amelioration of the Condition of Wounded, Sick and Shipwrecked Members of the Armed Forces at Sea (adopted August 12, 1949, entered into force October 21, 1950) (GC I), 75 UNTS 31, art. 47; Geneva Convention for the Amelioration of the Condition of Wounded, Sick and Shipwrecked Members of the Armed Forces in the Field (adopted August 12, 1949, entered into force October 21, 1950) (GC II), 75 UNTS 85, art. 48; Geneva Convention Relevant to the Treatment of Prisoners of War (adopted August 12, 1949, entered into force October 21, 1950) (GC III), 75 UNTS 135, art. 127; Geneva Convention Relevant to the Protection of Civilian Persons in Time of War (adopted August 12, 1949, entered into force October 21, 1950) (GC IV), 75 UNTS 287, art. 144.

12   GC III, art. 127.

13   Protocol Additional to the Geneva Conventions of 12 August 1949, and Relating to the Protection of Victims of International Armed Conflicts (adopted June 8, 1977, entered into force December 7, 1978) (AP I), 1125 UNTS 3, art. 83.

14   Ibid., art. 82.

15   Ibid., art. 87.

16   Julia Peristerakis, "Jody Williams and the Campaign to Ban Landmines," Canadian Museum for Human Rights, https://humanrights.ca/story/jody-williams-and-the-campaign-to-ban-landmines#:~:text=On%20October%2010%2C%20 1997%2C%20less,Ban%20Landmines%20and%20Jody%20Williams (accessed September 26, 2020).

17   Rome Statute of the International Criminal Court, July 17, 1998, 2187 UNTS 90, no. 38544.

18   Adam Roberts, "The Law of War: Problems of Implementation in Contemporary Conflicts," *Duke Journal of Comparative & International Law* 6 (1995): 70–72.

19   Rome Statute, art. 5.

20   Coalition for the International Criminal Court, "Special Edition, ICC Update," April 11, 2002, 1, 3, http://iccnow.org/documents/iccupdate26a.special.pdf.

21   BBC News, "Bosco Ntaganda Sentenced to 30 Years for Crimes in DR Congo," November 7, 2019, https://www.bbc.com/news/world-africa-50329503.

22   Stef Blok, "The International Criminal Court Must Do Better. Reforms Are Urgently Needed," *Washington Post*, December 2, 2019, https://www.washingtonpost.com/opinions/2019/12/02/international-criminal-court-must-do-better-reforms-are-urgently-needed/.

23   Jennifer Hansler, "Pompeo Slams International Criminal Court Decision to Authorize Afghanistan War Crimes Investigation," CNN, March 5, 2020, https://www.cnn.com/2020/03/05/politics/icc-afghanistan-pompeo/index.html.

24   Richard Falk, "Opening the Other Eye: Charles Taylor and Selective Accountability," *Al Jazeera*, May 1, 2012, https://www.aljazeera.com/opinions/2012/5/1/opening-the-other-eye-charles-taylor-and-selective-accountability/.

25   Human Rights Watch, "Human Rights Watch Briefing Note for the Eighteenth Session of the International Criminal Court Assembly of States Parties," November 1, 2019, https://www.hrw.org/sites/default/files/news_attachments/asp_final_en_0.pdf.

26   UN Office on Genocide Prevention and the Responsibility to Protect Project, "Responsibility to Protect," https://www.un.org/en/genocideprevention/about-responsibility-to-protect.shtml (accessed September 26, 2020).

27   International Commission on Intervention and State Sovereignty, *The Responsibility to Protect: Report of the International Commission on Intervention and State Sovereignty* (Ottawa: International Development Research Centre, 2001).

28   Ibid., xi.

29   UN General Assembly resolution 60/1, "2005 World Summit Outcome," A/RES/60/1, September 16, 2005, https://documents-dds-ny.un.org/doc/UNDOC/GEN/N05/487/60/pdf/N0548760.pdf?OpenElement.

30   Jody M. Prescott, "The North Atlantic Treaty Organization," in *An Institutional Approach to the Responsibility to Protect*, ed. Gentian Zyberi (London: Cambridge University Press, 2014), 348.

31   UN Security Council resolution 1973, "On the Situation in the Libyan Arab Jamahiriya," S/RES/1973. March 17, 2011.

32   Sarah Brockmeier, Oliver Stuenkel, and Marcos Tourinho, "The Impact of the Libya Intervention Debates on Norms of Protection," *Global Society* 30, no. 1 (2015): 121.

33   Peter Baker, "For Obama, Syria Chemical Attack Shows Risk of 'Deals with Dictators,'" *New York Times*, April 9, 2017, https://www.nytimes.com/2017/04/09/us/politics/obama-syria-chemical-weapons.html.

34   Brockmeier et al., "The Impact of the Libya Intervention Debates on Norms of Protection," 115.

35   Jody M. Prescott, "Litigating Genocide: A Consideration of the International Criminal Court in Light of the German Jews' Legal Response to Nazi Persecution, 1933–1941," *Maine Law Review* 51 (1999): 337–38.

36   Ibid., 337.

37   Rossi, "Training Armed Forces in IHL."

38   Tim Golden, "Years After 2 Afghans Died, Abuse Case Falters," *New York Times*, February 13, 2006, https://www.nytimes.com/2006/02/13/us/years-after-2-afghans-died-abuse-case-falters.html; John C. Dehn, "Institutional Advocacy, Constitutional Obligations, and Professional Responsibilities: Arguments for Government Lawyering without Glasses," *Columbia Law Review Sidebar* 110 (2010): 86–87.

39   *The U.S. Army in the Iraq War, Volume 1: Invasion–Insurgency–Civil War*, ed. Joel D. Rayburn and Frank K. Sobchak (Carlisle Barracks, PA: US Army War College Press, 2019), 311–12.

40   Charlie Savage and Elisabeth Bumiller, "An Iraqi Massacre, a Light Sentence, and a Question of Military Justice," *New York Times*, January 27, 2012, https://www.nytimes.com/2012/01/28/us/an-iraqi-massacre-a-light-sentence-and-a-question-of-military-justice.html; Anna Mulrine, "Pentagon Had Red Flags about Command Climate in 'Kill Team' Stryker Brigade," *Christian Science Monitor*, October 28, 2010, https://www.csmonitor.com/USA/Military/2010/1028/Pentagon-had-red-flags-about-command-climate-in-kill-team-Stryker-brigade.

41   Independent Institute for Administration and Civil Society Studies, "Public Opinion in Iraq, First Poll Following Abu Ghraib Revelations," June 15, 2004, https://www.globalpolicy.org/invasion-and-war/iraqi-public-opinion-and-polls.html.

42   Mark Boal, "The Kill Team: How U.S. Soldiers in Afghanistan Murdered Innocent Civilians," *Rolling Stone*, March 28, 2011, https://www.rollingstone.com/politics/politics-news/the-kill-team-how-u-s-soldiers-in-afghanistan-murdered-innocent-civilians-169793/.

43   Paul Daley, "Brereton War Crimes Report Fallout: What Now for Australia's Elite Special Forces?," *The Guardian*, November 19, 2020, https://www.theguardian.com/australia-news/2020/nov/19/brereton-war-crimes-report-fallout-what-now-for-australias-elite-special-forces.

44   Clyde H. Farnsworth, "Canada Ends Top Regiment after Charges," *New York Times*, January 25, 1995, A7.

45   Denielle Brassil, "Increasing Compliance with International Humanitarian Law through Dissemination," *University of Western Australia Law Review* 39, no. 1 (2015): 89–96.

46   Laurie R. Blank and Gregory P. Noone, *Law of War Training, Resources for Military and Civilian Leaders*, 2nd ed. (Washington, DC: United States Institute of Peace Press, 2013); David Lloyd Roberts, "Teaching the Law of Armed Conflict to Armed Forces: Personal Reflections," *International Law Studies* 82 (2006): 122–34.

Chapter 1 ICRC's Evolving Approach to IHL Training

1   Georges Willemin and Roger Heacock, *The International Committee of the Red Cross, International Organization and the Evolution of World Society, Vol. 2* (The Hague: Martinus Nijhoff, 1984), 19–27; Jean-Marie Henckaerts and Louise Doswald-Beck, *Customary International Law, Volume I: Rules* (Cambridge: Cambridge University Press, 2005), xxvi.

2   Yves Sandoz, "The International Committee of the Red Cross as Guardian of International Humanitarian Law," ICRC, December 31, 1998, https://www.icrc.org/en/doc/resources/documents/misc/about-the-icrc-311298.htm#:~:text=Article%205%20of%20the%20Statutes,alleged%20breaches%20of%20that%20law%E2%80%9D%20.

3   Statutes of the International Committee of the Red Cross, adopted on December 21, 2017, entered into force January 1, 2018, art. 4.1(g), 2017, https://www.icrc.org/en/document/statutes-international-committee-red-cross-0#:~:text=The%20ICRC%20is%20an%20association,in%20carrying%20out%20its%20work.

4   Elizabeth Stubbins Bates, "Towards Effective Military Training in International Humanitarian Law," *International Review of the Red Cross* 96, nos. 895/896 (2014): 796–99.

5   Greenberg Research, "The People on War Report, ICRC Worldwide Consultation on the Rules of War," October 1999, iii, 87, https://www.icrc.org/en/doc/assets/files/other/globalreport.pdf.

6   Ibid., 29.

7   Ibid., 34.

8   Ibid., 33–34.

9   WIN/Gallup International Association, "In Depth: Topics A to Z, Religion," https://news.gallup.com/poll/1690/religion.aspx (accessed July 26, 2020).

10   Greenberg Research, "The People on War Report," 62.

11   Daniel Muñoz-Rojas and Jean-Jacques Frésard, "The Roots of Behaviour in War: Understanding and Preventing IHL Violations," *International Review of the Red Cross* 853 (March 2004): 190–91.

12   Ibid., 191–92.

13   Ibid., 196.

14   Ibid., 193–94.

15   Ibid., 196–200.

16   Ibid., 203–4.

17   Ibid., 206.

18   Greg Jaffe, "The Cursed Platoon," *Washington Post*, July 2, 2020, https://www.washingtonpost.com/graphics/2020/national/clint-lorance-platoon-afghanistan/.

19   Patrick Oppman, "Soldier Found Guilty of Murdering Afghans, Sentenced to Life," CNN, November 11, 2011, https://www.cnn.com/2011/11/10/justice/soldier-murder--rial/index.html.

20   Christopher Knaus, "Australian Special Forces Involved in Murder of 39 Afghan Civilians, War Crimes Report Alleges," *The Guardian*, November 19, 2020, https://www.theguardian.com/australia-news/2020/nov/19/australian-special-forces-involved-in-of-39-afghan-civilians-war-crimes-report-alleges.

21   George R. Mastroanni, "The Person-Situation Debate: Implications for Military Leadership and Civil-Military Relations," *Journal of Military Ethics* 10, no. 1 (2011): 11.

22   ICRC, *Integrating the Law, Publication Ref. 0900* (Geneva: ICRC, May 2007), 1, 17–35, https://www.icrc.org/en/doc/assets/files/other/icrc-002-0900.pdf

23 Emanuele Castano, Bernhard Leidner, and Patrycja Slawuta, "Social Identification Processes, Group Dynamics and the Behaviour of Combatants," *International Review of the Red Cross* 90, no. 870 (June 2008): 260, 271.

24 Dale Stephens, "Behaviour in War: The Place of Law, Moral Inquiry and Self-Identity," *International Review of the Red Cross*, 96, nos. 895/896 (2014): 752–53.

25 Ibid., 757.

26 Fiona Terry and Brian McQuinn, *The Roots of Restraint in War* (Geneva: ICRC, 2018), 6, 12.

27 Ibid., 29.

28 Ibid.

29 Inspector-General of the Australian Defence Force, *Afghanistan Inquiry Report* (Canberra: I-GADF, 2020), 28–36.

30 Ibid., 29, 30.

31 Ibid., 31.

32 Ibid.

33 Andrew M. Bell and Fionna Terry, "Combatant Rank and Socialization to Norms of Restraint: Examining the Australian and Philippine Armies," *International Interactions* 59, no. 4 (2021): 11–14.

34 Ibid., 14–15.

35 Ibid., 15–17.

36 Ibid., 17–18.

37 Ibid., 18–20.

38 Ibid., 21.

39 Jody M. Prescott, "Training in the Law of Armed Conflict—A NATO Perspective," *Journal of Military Ethics* 7, no. 1 (March 2008): 66–75.

40 Bell and Terry, "Combatant Rank and Socialization," 23–24.

41 Terry and McQuinn, *The Roots of Restraint*, 31, 32–33, 34.

42 Ibid., 9, 28, 29, 34, 68.

43 Ibid., 9, 29, 68.

44 Ibid., 9.

45 See Reuters, "EA Profit, Revenue Top Estimates on Strong 'Battlefield 1' Sales," January 31, 2017, https://www.reuters.com/article/us-electronic-arts-results/ea-profit-revenue-top-estimates-on-strong-battlefield-1-sales-idUSKBN15F2LQ.

46 Gary Brown, Daniel Greenberg, Seth Hudson, and Kurt Sanger, "Rules of the (Video) Game: IHL on the Virtual Battlefield," *American Society of International Law Proceedings* 109 (2015): 55–61.

47 James Batchelor, "Can Video Games Depict War Responsibly?," Gamesindustry.biz, May 7, 2020, https://www.gamesindustry.biz/articles/2020-05-07-war-and-video-games.

48 C. J. Robles, "New Survey Finds 75% of Gamers Play Video Games to Maintain Mental Health," *Tech Times*, October 22, 2020, https://www.techtimes.com/articles/253551/20201022/new-survey-finds-75-gamers-play-video-games-maintain-mental.htm.

49 Alex Miller, "How Video Games Are Saving Those Who Served," *Wired*, October 20, 2020, https://www.wired.com/story/video-games-therapy-veterans-ptsd-treatment/.

50 Brock Bastian, Jolanda Jetten, and Helena R. M. Radke, "Cyber-Dehumanization: Violent Video Game Play Diminishes Our Humanity," *Journal of Experimental Social Psychology* 48 (2012): 489–90.

51 Jose Antonio Vargas, "Virtual Reality Prepares Soldiers for Real War Young Warriors Say Video Shooter Games Helped Hone Their Skills," *Washington Post*, February 14, 2006, https://www.washingtonpost.com/archive/politics/2006/02/14/virtual-reality-prepares-soldiers-for-real-war-span-classbankheadyoung-warriors-say-video-shooter-games-helped-hone-their-skillsspan/15996806-3a4d-4374-b066-38c5f5c35659/.

52 Sarah McCammon, "The Warfare May Be Remote But the Trauma Is Real," *NPR*, April 24, 2017, https://www.npr.org/2017/04/24/525413427/for-drone-pilots-warfare-may-be-remote-but-the-trauma-is-real.

53 WIN/Gallup International Association, "People on War—2016 Survey," 2016, https://www.icrc.org/en/document/people-war-2016-background-and-methodology.

54 Ibid., 74, 76.

55 Ibid., 110.

56 Ibid., 84.

57 ICRC, *Millennials on War*, Publication Ref. 4444 (Geneva: ICRC, January 2020), 11–12, https://shop.icrc.org/millennials-on-war-pdf-en.

Chapter 2 Command & General Staff College Class of 2002

1 US Army Command and General Staff College, "Law of War and Rules of Engagement Training Survey, No. 02-004," 2001 (copy of the approved survey instrument and the results of the survey on file with author).

2 Thomas E. Creviston, email message to author, January 20, 2021.

3 Huba Wass deCzege, "The School of Advanced Military Studies: An Accident of History," *Military Review* 89, no. 4 (July–August 2009): 102–3.

4 Memorandum for Chief, DAD, CGSC, from LTC Jody M. Prescott, subject: Request for CGSC Research Control Number, September 6, 2001 (copy on file with author).

5 Neal H. Bralley, "ILE: A New System for CGSC Students," *Army Logistician* 38, no. 1 (January/February 2006), https://alu.army.mil/alog/issues/JanFeb06/ile_cgsc.html.

6 Kimberly Jackson, Katherine L. Kidder, Sean Mann, William H. Waggy II, Natasha Lander, and S. Rebecca Zimmerman, *Raising the Flag: Implications of U.S. Military Approaches to General and Flag Officer Development* (Santa Monica, CA: RAND Corporation, 2020), xxi–xxii, 182, 203–4.

7 CGSC, "Law of War and Rules of Engagement Training Survey."

8 Ibid.

9 Ibid.

10 Ibid.

11 US Department of Defense, "Military Units, Army," https://www.defense.gov/Experience/Military-Units/Army/ (accessed August 17, 2020).

12 Headquarters, Department of the Army (HQDA), *Army Regulation 600-20, Army Command Policy* (Washington, DC: HQDA, 2006), 11.

13 CGSC, "Law of War and Rules of Engagement Training Survey."

14 US General Accounting Office, "Military Readiness: Full Training Benefits from Army's Combat Training Centers Are Not Being Realized, GAO/NSIAD-99-210," September 1999, 1–9, https://www.gao.gov/assets/230/228237.pdf.

15 Ibid., 4.

16 CGSC, "Law of War and Rules of Engagement Training Survey."

17 Ibid.

18   Ibid.

19   Ibid.

20   Ibid.

21   Ibid.

22   Ibid.

23   Ibid.

24   Ibid.

25   Ibid.

26   Ibid.

27   Jody M. Prescott and Jerry Dunlap, "Law of War and Rules of Engagement Training for the Objective Force: A Proposed Methodology for Training Role-Players," *Army Lawyer* (July 2000): 47.

28   Anita Stratton, "Roleplayers and Technology Enhance Soldier Training," *Defense Visual Information Distribution Service*, August 24, 2015, https://www.dvidshub.net/news/174262/roleplayers-and-technology-enhance-soldier-training.

29   CGSC, "Law of War and Rules of Engagement Training Survey."

30   "IHL Database, Rule 140. Principle of Reciprocity," ICRC, https://ihl-databases. icrc.org/customary-ihl/eng/docs/v1_rul_rule140 (accessed November 21, 2020).

31   HQDA and Headquarters, United States Marine Corps (HUSMC), *Field Manual 27-10/Marine Corps Tactical Publication 11-10C, The Commander's Handbook on the Law of Land Warfare* (Washington, DC: HQDA and HUSMC, 2019), 8-1; "Law of Armed Conflict, Basic Knowledge, Lesson 1," International Committee of the Red Cross, 2002, 5-1, https://www.icrc.org/en/doc/assets/files/other/law1_final.pdf.

32   CGSC, "Law of War and Rules of Engagement Survey."

33   Ibid.

34   Ibid.

35   Ibid.

36   Ibid.

37   Ibid.

38   Ibid.

39   Ibid.

40   Richard Luscombe, "Navy Seal Pardoned of War Crimes by Trump Described by Colleagues as 'freaking evil,'" *The Guardian*, December 27, 2019, https://www.theguardian.com/us-news/2019/dec/27/eddie-gallagher-trump-navy-seal-iraq.

41   David K. Aragon, "The Challenge of Surviving within the Special Operations Culture," in *Case Studies of Operational Culture*, ed. Paula Holmes-Eber and Marcus J. Mainz (Quantico, VA: Marine Corps University Press, 2014), 7.

42   Ibid., 8.

43   Patrick Paterson, *Training Surrogate Forces in International Humanitarian Law: Lessons from Peru, Colombia, El Salvador, and Iraq, JSOU Report 16-9* (Tampa, FL: Joint Special Operations University Press, 2016); Todd Burkhart and Rob Williamson, "Incorporating Law of Armed Conflict Training into Afghanistan's Special Forces' Curriculum," *Army Press Online Journal* 16, no. 15 (2016): 1–7, https://www.armyupress.army.mil/Journals/Military-Review/Online-Exclusive/2016-Online-Exclusive-Articles/Incorporating-Law-of-Armed-Conflict-Training/.

44   Anja Dalgaard-Nielsen and Kirstine Falster Holm, "Supersoldiers or Rulebreakers? Unpacking the Mind-Set of Special Operations Forces," *Armed Forces & Society* 45, no. 4 (2019): 594–95.

45   I-GADF, *Afghanistan Inquiry Report*, 110.
46   Mastroanni, "The Person-Situation Debate," 11.
47   CGSC, "Law of War and Rules of Engagement Survey."
48   Ibid.
49   Antonio M. Taguba, *AR 15-6 Investigation of the 800th Military Police Brigade* (Baghdad: Coalition Forces Land Component Command, 2004), 19, https://www.thetorturedatabase.org/document/ar-15-6-investigation-800th-military-police-investigating-officer-mg-antonio-taguba-taguba-.
50   CGSC, "Law of War and Rules of Engagement Training Survey."
51   Ibid.
52   Ibid.
53   Ibid.
54   David Fitzgerald, "Vietnam, Iraq and the Rebirth of Counter-Insurgency," *Irish Studies in International Affairs* 21 (2010): 151–54.
55   Meghan Keneally, "Why the US Got Involved in Afghanistan—And Why It's Been Difficult to Get Out," *ABC News*, 21 August 2017, https://abcnews.go.com/US/us-involved-afghanistan-difficult/story?id=49341264.
56   Daniel L. Magruder, *Counterinsurgency, Security Forces, and the Identification Problem: Distinguishing Friend from Foe* (London: Routledge, 2018), 1–2.
57   Jody M. Prescott, "Tactical Implementation of Rules of Engagement in a Multinational Force Reality," in *U.S. Military Operations: Law, Policy, and Practice*, ed. Geoffrey S. Corn, Rachel E. VanLandingham, and Shane R. Reeves (New York: Oxford University Press, 2016), 253, 256–58.
58   Bryan Frederick and David E. Johnson, *The Continued Evolution of U.S. Law of Armed Conflict Implementation* (Santa Monica, CA: RAND Corporation, 2015), 22.

Chapter 3   Battlefield IHL Compliance Assessment

1   Joel D. Rayburn and Frank K. Sobchak (eds.), *The U.S. Army in the Iraq War, Volume 1: Invasion–Insurgency–Civil War* (Carlisle Barracks, PA: US Army War College Press, 2019), 81–102.
2   Ibid., 118–559.
3   Ibid., 627–57; Nicholas J. Schlosser, *The Surge: 2007–2008* (Washington, DC: US Army Center of Military History, 2017), 7.
4   Schlosser, *The Surge: 2007–2008*, 30–88.
5   Office of the Surgeon, Multinational Force-Iraq, and Office of the Surgeon General, US Army Medical Command, *Mental Health Advisory Team (MHAT) IV, Operation Iraqi Freedom 05-07, Final Report*, November 17, 2006, 6, http://www.peaceispatriotic.org/articles/MHAT_IV_Report_17NOV06.pdf (hereafter MHAT-IV).
6   Office of the Surgeon General, US Army Medical Command; Office of the Command Surgeon, Headquarters, US Army Central Command; and Office of the Command Surgeon, US Forces Afghanistan, *Mental Health Advisory Team 9 (MHAT 9) Operation Enduring Freedom 2013, Afghanistan*, October 10, 2013, https://apps.dtic.mil/dtic/tr/fulltext/u2/a593777.pdf (hereafter MHAT 9).
7   Office of the Command Surgeon [redacted] and Office of the Surgeon General, US Army Medical Command, *Mental Health Advisory Team (MHAT) V, Operation Enduring Freedom 8, Afghanistan*, February 14, 2008, https://armymedicine.health.mil/Reports (hereafter MHAT V OEF).

8   Office of the Surgeon, Multi-National Force-Iraq, and Office of the Surgeon General, US Army Medical Command, *Mental Health Advisory Team (MHAT) V, Operation Iraqi Freedom 06-08* (MHAT V OIF), February 14, 2008, https://apps.dtic.mil/dtic/tr/fulltext/u2/a519676.pdf (hereafter MHAT V OIF).

9   MHAT V OEF, 144.

10 Ibid., 145, 148, 155, 157.

11 Ibid., 147.

12 Ibid.

13 Office of the Surgeon, Multinational Force-Iraq and Office of the Surgeon General, United States Army Medical Command, *Mental Health Advisory Team (MHAT) IV, Operation Iraqi Freedom 05-07, Final Report*, November 17, 2006, https://ntrl.ntis.gov/NTRL/dashboard/searchResults/titleDetail/PB2010103335.xhtml (hereafter MHAT IV).

14 MHAT V OEF, 157, 158.

15 Ibid., 181.

16 Ibid., 160.

17 CBS News, "Whiskey and Golf before Rape-Murder?" August 7, 2006, https://www.cbsnews.com/news/whiskey-and-golf-before-rape-murder/; BBC News, "US Soldier Admits Murdering Girl," February 22, 2007, http://news.bbc.co.uk/2/hi/americas/6384781.stm.

18 William Yardley, "Drug Use Cited in the Killings of 3 Civilians: Testimony in Afghan Case—Tapes Aired," *New York Times*, September 28, 2010, A1; William Yardley, "Soldier Is Given 24 Years in Civilian Afghan Deaths," *New York Times*, March 24, 2011, A20.

19 MHAT V OEF, 160, 161.

20 Ibid., 160, 161.

21 Ibid.

22 Ibid., 161.

23 Ibid., 162.

24 Christopher H. Warner, George N. Appenzeller, Angela Mobbs, Jessica R. Parker, Carolynn M. Warner, Thomas Grieger, and Charles W. Hoge, "Effectiveness of Battlefield-Ethics Training during Combat Deployment: A Programme Assessment," *Lancet* 378 (2011): 923.

25 Julie A. Schumacher and Kenneth E. Leonard, "Husbands' and Wives' Marital Adjustment, Verbal Aggression, and Physical Aggression as Longitudinal Predictors of Physical Aggression in Early Marriage," *Journal of Consulting and Clinical Psychology* 73, no. 1 (2005): 28–29.

26 MHAT V OEF, 162.

27 Ibid.

28 Ibid., 163.

29 Michael N. Schmitt, "Investigating Violations of International Law in Armed Conflict," *Harvard National Security Journal* 2 (2011): 36–37.

30 GC III, art. 130.

31 Schmitt, "Investigating Violations of International Law in Armed Conflict," 40–43.

32 Office of the General Counsel of the Department of Defense, Department of Defense Directive 2311.01, "DoD Law of War Program," July 2, 2020, 3, 13, 15.

33 MHAT V OEF, 175.

34 Ibid.

35 Headquarters, Department of the Army (HQDA), *Army Regulation (AR) 350-1, Army Training and Leader Development* (Washington, DC: HQDA, 2017), 188.

36 MHAT V OEF, 176.

37 Ibid., 176, 177.

38 See HQDA, *AR 350-1, Army Training and Leader Development* (Washington, DC: HQDA, 2007), 81.

39 Ibid., 177.

40 Ibid., 164.

41 Ibid., 164, 165.

42 Ibid., 169.

43 MHAT V OIF, 42.

44 Ibid.

45 MHAT V OEF, 169.

46 Ibid., 169, 170.

47 Office of the Surgeon General, US Army Medical Command; Office of the Command Surgeon, HQ, USCENTCOM; and Office of the Command Surgeon, US Forces Afghanistan (USFOR-A), *Joint Mental Health Advisory Team 7 (J-MHAT 7), Operation Enduring Freedom 2020, Afghanistan* (J-MHAT 7), February 22, 2011, 29, https://armymedicine.health.mil/Reports.

48 Jim Garamone, "Noncommissioned Officers Give Big Advantage to U.S. Military," Defense, November 7, 2019, https://www.defense.gov/Explore/News/Article/Article/2011393/noncommissioned-officers-give-big-advantage-to-us-military/#:~:text=%22NCOs%20are%20the%20doers%2C%22,of%20those%20in%20their%20charge.%22.

49 C. Todd Lopez, "Study Focuses on Mental Health of Force in Afghanistan," US Army, May 20, 2011, https://www.army.mil/article/56845/study_focuses_on_mental_health_of_force_in_afghanistan.

50 MHAT V OEF, 169.

51 MHAT V OIF, 48.

52 Ibid.

53 MHAT V OEF, 172.

54 A. Nyberg, L. Alfredsson, T. Theorell, H. Westerlund, J. Vahtera, and M. Kivimäki, "Managerial Leadership and Ischaemic Heart Disease Among Employees: The Swedish WOLF Study," *Occupational and Environmental Medicine* 66, no. 1 (January 2009): 51.

55 E. Kevin Kelloway, Nick Turner, Julian Barling, and Catherine Loughlin, "Transformational Leadership and Employee Psychological Well-being: The Mediating Role of Employee Trust in Leadership," *Work & Stress* 26, no. 1 (January–March 2012): 42.

56 MHAT V OEF, 172.

57 Ibid.

58 Morten Nordmo, Olav Kjellevold Olsen, Jørn Hetland, Roar Espevik, Arnold Bastiaan Bakker, and Ståle Pallesen, "Daily Sleep Quality and Naval Work Performance: The Role of Leadership," *International Maritime Health* 70, no. 4 (2019): 207.

59 MHAT V OEF, 182.

60 MHAT V OIF, 64.

61 Christopher H. Warner and George Appenzeller, "Engaged Leadership—Linking the Professional Ethic and Battlefield Behaviors," *Military Review* 91 (September–October 2011): 63.

62 Roper Center for Public Opinion Research, "American Soldiers Studies of WWII," https://ropercenter.cornell.edu/american-soldiers-studies-wwii (accessed August 21, 2020).

63 Samuel A. Stouffer, "Men from the 101st Airborne, European Theater of Operations," Research Branch, Information and Education Division, War Department, May 1944, 12–13, https://ropercenter.cornell.edu/ipoll/study/31089936.

64 David E. Jones, Franca Jones, Laura Suttinger, Ayessa Toler, Patricia Hammond, and Steven Medina, "Placement of Combat Stress Teams in Afghanistan: Reducing Barriers to Care," *Military Medicine* 178, no. 2 (2013): 121–22.

65 Warner and Appenzeller, "Engaged Leadership," 63.

66 MHAT V OEF, 161.

67 MHAT IV, 42.

Chapter 4 Battlefield Ethics Training in Iraq

1 Christopher H. Warner and George Appenzeller, "Engaged Leadership: Linking the Professional Ethic and Battlefield Behaviors," *Military Review* 91, no. 5 (September–October 2011): 63.

2 Ibid.

3 Christopher H. Warner, George N. Appenzeller, Angela Mobbs, Jessica R. Parker, Carolynn M. Warner, Thomas Grieger, and Charles W. Hoge, "Effectiveness of Battlefield Ethics Training during Combat Deployment," *Lancet* 378 (September 2011): 916–17.

4 Ibid., 916.

5 Ibid.

6 Ibid., 918, 919–20.

7 Ibid., 917–18.

8 Ibid., 917.

9 Jay Sharbutt, "'Platoon' Is Top Film; Newman Is Best Actor," *Los Angeles Times*, March 31, 1987, https://www.latimes.com/archives/la-xpm-1987-03-31-mn-1504-story.html

10 Library of Congress, "Brief Descriptions and Expanded Essays of National Film Registry Titles," https://www.loc.gov/programs/national-film-preservation-board/film-registry/descriptions-and-essays/ (accessed September 6, 2020).

11 Warner et al., "Effectiveness of Battlefield Ethics Training," 917.

12 Ibid.

13 Ibid., 920.

14 Ibid., 921.

15 Ibid., 920.

16 Ibid.

17 Ibid., 921.

18 Ibid., 921, 922.

19 Darren W. Holowka, Erika J. Wolf, Brian P. Marx, Kristen M. Foley, Danny G. Kaloupek, and Terence M. Keane, "Associations among Personality, Combat Exposure and Wartime Atrocities," *Psychology of Violence* 2, no. 3 (2012): 263–69.

20 Warner et al., "Effectiveness of Battlefield Ethics Training," 922.

21 Ibid.

22 Warner and Appenzeller, "Engaged Leadership," 69.

23 Department of Defense, *Law of War Manual*, 15–16.

24 Adjutant-General's Office, US War Department, *General Orders No. 100, Instructions for the Government of Armies of the United States in the Field* (New York: D. van Nostrand, 1863), 10, https://archive.org/details/governarmies00unitrich/page/10/mode/2up.

25 Headquarters, Department of the Army (HQDA), *Field Manual 27-10, The Law of Land Warfare* (Washington, DC: HQDA, 1956), 3.

26 Wallach, "Pray Fire First Gentlemen of France," 463.

27 ICRC, "Fundamentals of IHL," https://casebook.icrc.org/law/fundamentals-ihl# (accessed November 24, 2020).

28 HQDA, *ADP 6-22 C1, Army Leadership and the Profession* (Washington, DC: HQDA, 2019), v.

29 Ibid., ix.

30 Ibid., 2-1–2-5.

31 Ibid., 1-4.

32 Ibid., 2-8.

33 Chris Jenks, "The Efficacy of the U.S. Army's Law of War Training Program," Articles of War (blog), Lieber Institute at West Point, October 14, 2020, https://lieber.westpoint.edu/efficacy-u-s-armys-law-of-war-training-program/.

34 HQDA, *Army Regulation (AR) 350-1, Army Training and Leader Development* (Washington, DC: HQDA, 2017), 26.

35 Ibid., table F-2, 188.

36 See HQDA, *AR 350-1, Army Training and Leader Development* (Washington, DC: HQDA, 2007), 81.

37 HQDA, *AR 350-1, Army Training and Leader Development*, 2017, table F-2, 188.

38 Richard P. DiMeglio, "Training Army Judge Advocates to Advise Commanders as Operational Law Attorneys," *Boston College Law Review* 54, no. 3 (2013): 1191.

39 Ibid., 1185–206.

40 Victor M. Hansen, "Developing Empirical Methodologies to Study Law of War Violations," *Willamette Journal of International Law and Dispute Resolution* 16, no. 2 (2008): 346.

41 Ibid., 344, 383–84, 357–59.

42 Ibid. 360–68.

43 Ibid. 369–70.

44 Laura A. Dickinson, "Military Lawyers on the Battlefield: An Empirical Account of International Law Compliance," *American Journal of International Law* 104, no. 1 (2010): 5.

45 Ibid., 15.

46 Ibid., 11n57, 15.

47 Richard D. Rosen, "The Judge Advocate General's School, U.S. Army: 50 Years in Charlottesville," *Virginia Lawyer* (December 2001): 16.

48 Ibid., 3, 8, 17, 27–28.

49 I-GADF, *Afghanistan Inquiry Report*, 36, 420–50.

50 Joseph Doty and Joe Gelineau, "Command Climate," *Army Magazine* 58, no. 7 (July 2008): 22–23, https://www.ausa.org/sites/default/files/FC_Doty_0708.pdf.

51 US Army G-1, Personnel, "Army Command Climate Survey: Soldiers in TO&E Units, ver. 6.2," https://www.armyg1.army.mil/documents/CMD_Climate_Surveys/TOE-CCSv6.2%2006_2013.pdf (accessed August 23, 2020).

52 Erik Slavin, "Navy Medicine CO Fired for Poor Command Climate," Stars and Stripes, April 12, 2012, https://www.stripes.com/navy-medicine-co-fired-for-poor-command-climate-1.174217#:~:text=YOKOSUKA%20NAVAL%20BASE%2C%20Japan%20%E2%80%94%20The,April%206%20by%20Rear%20Adm.

53 S. Ananthan and S. Inderjit, "Evaluating the Command Climate in Military Units," *European Journal of Educational Sciences* 1, no. 3 (September 2014): 167.

54 Christopher H. Warner, email to author, July 16, 2020.

55 Joshua E. Wilk, Paul D. Bliese, Jeffrey L. Thomas, Michael D. Wood, Dennis McGurk, Carl A. Castro, and Charles W. Hoge, "Unethical Battlefield Conduct Reported by Soldiers Serving in the Iraq War," *Journal of Nervous and Mental Disease* 201, no. 4 (2013): 263.

56 Ibid.

57 Ibid.

58 Deidre MacManus, Kimberlie Dean, Margaret Jones, Roberto J. Rona, Neil Greenberg, Lisa Hull, Tom Fahy, Simon Wessely, and Nicola T. Fear, "Violent Offending by UK Military Personnel Deployed to Iraq and Afghanistan: A Data Linkage Cohort Study," *Lancet* 381 (2013): 910–11.

59 Ibid., 908, 913–15.

60 The Judge Advocate General's Legal Center and School (TJAGLCS), *Commander's Legal Handbook, Misc. Pub. 27-8* (Charlottesville, VA: TJAGSLC, 2019), 294, 301.

61 Ibid., 300.

62 Jenks, "The Efficacy of the U.S. Army's Law of War Program."

63 HQDA and Headquarters, United States Marine Corps (HUSMC), *Field Manual 6-27/MCTP 11-10C, Change 1, The Commander's Handbook on the Law of Land Warfare* (Washington, DC: HQDA and HUSMC, September 2019).

64 Ibid., 1-8, 1-28.

65 Ibid., vii, 1-16.

66 Laurie R. Blank, "Examining the Role of Law of War Training in International Criminal Accountability," *Utah Law Review* 2017, no. 4, article 6 (2017): 756–69.

67 Melissa de White, "In a War Perceived as Just, Many Americans Excuse Soldiers Who Commit War Crimes, Stanford Scholar Finds," *Stanford News*, December 9, 2019, https://news.stanford.edu/2019/12/09/war-perceived-just-many-americans-excuse-war-criminals/.

68 Jaffe, "The Cursed Platoon," *Washington Post*, July 2, 2020, https://www.washingtonpost.com/podcasts/post-reports/the-cursed-platoon-part-1/.

69 Falih Hassan and Jane Arraf, "Blackwater's Bullets Scarred Iraqis. Trump's Pardon Renewed the Pain," *New York Times*, December 23, 2020, https://www.nytimes.com/2020/12/23/world/middleeast/blackwater-trump-pardon.html.

70 "Meet the Participants, My Lai," PBS, https://www.pbs.org/wgbh/americanexperience/features/my-lai-selected-men-involved-my-lai/ (accessed November 24, 2020).

71 Charlie Savage and Elisabeth Bumiller, "An Iraqi Massacre, a Light Sentence and a Question of Military Justice," *New York Times*, January 27, 2012, https://www.newyorktimes.com/2012/01/28/us/an-iraqi-massacre-a-light-sentence-and-a-question-of-military-justice.html.

72 J. F. R. Boddens Hosang, *Rules of Engagement and the International Law of Military Operations* (New York: Oxford University Press, 2020), 250–52.

73 Ibid., 241, 253.
74 Alon Margalit, *Investigating Civilian Casualties in Times of Armed Conflict and Belligerent Occupation: Manoeuvring between Legal Regimes and Paradigms for the Use of Force* (Leiden: Brill Nijhoff, 2018), 23–47, 48–76, 153–223.
75 Mastroanni, "The Person-Situation Debate," 9.
76 Jenks, "The Efficacy of the U.S. Army's Law of War Training Program."
77 Office of the General Counsel, Department of Defense Directive 2311.01, DoD Law of War Program, 3 (July 2, 2020), https://www.esd.whs.mil/Portals/54/Documents/DD/issuances/dodd/231101p.pdf?ver=2020-07-02-143157-007.

Chapter 5 Education and Training Case Studies

1 Dale Stephens, "Behaviour in War: The Place of Law, Moral Inquiry and Self-Identity," *International Review of the Red Cross* 96, nos. 895–96 (2014): 761–62.
2 Megan M. Thompson and Rakesh Jetly, "Battlefield Ethics Training: Integrating Ethical Scenarios in High-Intensity Military Field Exercises," *European Journal of Psychotraumatology* 5, no. 1 (2014): 1.
3 Stefan Seiler, Andreas Fischer, and Sibylle A. Voegtli, "Developing Moral Decision-Making Competence: A Quasi-Experimental Intervention Study in the Swiss Armed Forces," *Ethics and Behavior* 21, no. 6 (2011): 452.
4 Christopher M. Barnes, John Schaubroeck, Megan Huth, and Sonia Ghumman, "Lack of Sleep and Unethical Conduct," *Organizational Behavior and Human Decision Processes* 115 (2011): 171–73.
5 Olav Kjellevold Olsen, Ståle Pallesen, and Jarle Eid, "The Impact of Partial Sleep Deprivation on Moral Reasoning in Military Officers," *SLEEP* 33 no. 8 (2010): 1087.
6 Ibid.
7 Ibid.
8 Olav Kjellevold Olsen, email to author, January 9, 2021.
9 Olsen et al., "The Impact of Partial Sleep Deprivation," 1088–89.
10 Ibid., 1089.
11 Seiler, "Developing Moral Decision-Making Competence,", 459
12 Ibid.
13 Ibid., 458.
14 Ibid., 460.
15 Ibid., 457–58.
16 Ibid., 458.
17 Ibid., 459–60.
18 Ibid., 461.
19 Ibid., 464–65.
20 Ibid., 465.
21 Ibid.
22 Eva van Baarle, Laura Hartman, Desiree Verweij, Bert Molewijk, and Guy Widdershoven, "What Sticks? The Evaluation of a Train-the-Trainer Course in Military Ethics and Its Perceived Outcomes," *Journal of Military Ethics* 16, no. 1–2 (2017): 74.
23 Seiler et al., "Developing Moral Decision-Making," 465.
24 Stefan Seiler, LinkedIn message to author, July 29, 2020.

25 Beyond Peace, www.beyondpeace.fr.

26 Cynthia Petrigh, interview with Jody M. Prescott, August 13, 2020.

27 Cynthia Petrigh, *Even Wars Have Limits: An IHL Training Manual, Based on the Training Designed and Delivered for the European Union Training Mission in Mali (EUTM), Koulikouro Training Camp* (Paris: Beyond Peace, 2014), 11.

28 Petrigh interview.

29 Ibid.

30 Ibid.

31 Petrigh, *Even Wars Have Limits*, 50.

32 Petrigh interview.

33 Ibid.

34 Emily Knowles and Jahara Matisek, "Is Human Rights Training Working with Foreign Militaries? No One Knows and That's O.K.," War on the Rocks, May 12, 2020, https://waronthcrocks.com/2020/05/is-human-rights-training-working-with-foreign-militaries-no-one-knows-and-thats-o-k/.

35 Brian Ketz and Jody Prescott, "Ordinary Soldiers," Legacy of Learning Series, Norwich University, April 29, 2020, https://attendee.gotowebinar.com/recording/67643461427341839 (webinar ID 576-589-243).

36 Evan Kowalski and Jody M. Prescott, "Hybrid Conflict and Effective Leadership Training," *Journal of Military Learning* 3, no. 2 (October 2019): 82, https://www.armyupress.army.mil/Journals/Journal-of-Military-Learning/Journal-of-Military-Learning-Archives/October-2019/Kowalski-hybrid-conflict/.

37 David Frey, Waitman Beorn, Jennifer Ciardelli, Gretchen Skidmore, and Jody Prescott, *Ordinary Soldiers: A Study in Ethics, Law, and Leadership* (Washington, DC: United States Holocaust Memorial Museum and Center for Holocaust and Genocide Studies at West Point, 2014), https://www.ushmm.org/m/pdfs/20140830-ordinary-soldiers-case-study.pdf.

38 See LTC Ketz, Brian J., email to SFC Monica Garcia, subject "FEEDBACK Staff Ride 15-6, November 25, 2017" (copy on file with author).

39 Kowalski, "Hybrid Conflict," 88.

40 Evan Kowalski, "16th Special Troops 'Vanguard' Battalion Develops Leaders Through Innovative Curriculum, Staff Ride," US Army, December 28, 2017, https://www.army.mil/article/198488/.

41 Kowalski, "Hybrid Conflict," 89.

42 Ibid., 89–90.

43 ICRC, "Video Games That Protect Civilians," October 16, 2017, https://www.youtube.com/watch?v=0nSpXOAiYr8&feature=youtu.be.

44 "Red Cross Develops War Video Games—With Rules," March 19, 2019, https://www.youtube.com/watch?v=wQc4-vFJ2Oc.

45 ICRC, "Video Games and Law of War," September 27, 2013, https://www.icrc.org/en/document/video-games-get-real.

46 ICRC, "Let's Get Real," April 29, 2019, https://blogs.icrc.org/inspired/2019/04/29/half-bohemia-interactive-s-net-revenue-laws-war-dlc-2017-donated-icrc/.

47 Ibid.

48 Luke Moffett, Dug Cubie, and Andrew Godden, "Bringing the Battlefield into the Classroom: Using Video Games to Teach and Assess International Humanitarian Law," *Law Teacher* 51, no. 4 (2017).

49 Keisuke Minai, "Encouragement of Learning Through War Video Games as an Intelligible Textbook on International Humanitarian Law," *Cornell International Law Journal* 52 (2020).

50 Moffett et al., "Bringing the Battlefield into the Classroom," 508, 509, 510.

51 Ibid., 511, 512.

52 Ibid., 513.

53 Luke Moffett, email to author, August 11, 2020.

54 Minai, "Encouragement of Learning Through War Video Games," 646–48.

55 Ibid., 647n15.

56 Ibid., 647.

57 Ibid., 652–64.

58 Ibid., 652–53.

59 Keisuke Minai, email to author, August 13, 2020.

60 Minai, "Encouragement of Learning Through War Video Games," 657.

61 Minai, email to author, August 13, 2020.

62 Minai, "Encouragement of Learning Through War Video Games," 644.

63 Ibid., 668.

64 Keisuke Minai, email to author, November 26, 2020.

65 Minai, "Encouragement of Learning Through War Video Games," 670.

66 Keisuke Minai, email to author, August 12, 2020.

67 Minai, email to author, August 13, 2020.

68 Gary Brown, Daniel Greenberg, Seth Hudson and Kurt Sanger, "Rules of the (Video) Game: IHL on the Virtual Battlefield," *American Society of International Law Proceedings* 109 (2015): 56.

69 H. R. McMaster, "Preserving Soldiers' Moral Character in Counter-Insurgency Operations," in *Ethics Education for Irregular Warfare*, ed. Don Carrick, James Connelly, and Paul Robinson (Farnham: Ashgate, 2009), 16–21.

70 Jenks, "The Efficacy of the U.S. Army's Law of War Training Program."

71 Olav Kjellevold Olsen, email to author, January 9, 2021.

72 Matthew Talbert and Jessica Wolfendale, *War Crimes: Causes, Excuses, and Blame* (New York: Oxford University Press, 2019), 152.

73 I-GADF, *Afghanistan Inquiry Report*, 110.

74 Ibid., 37–42.

75 Cynthia Petrigh, email to author, August 24, 2020.

76 Talbert and Wolfendale, *War Crimes*, 152.

Conclusion

1 BBC News, "Royal Navy's First Crewless Boat Ready for Testing," June 24, 2020, https://www.bbc.com/news/uk-53161264.

2 Rupert Smith, *The Utility of Force: The Art of War in the Modern World* (New York: Knopf, 2007), xiii, 269–307.

3 Marc Fisher, Meagan Flynn, Jessica Contrera, and Carol D. Leonnig, "The Four-Hour Insurrection: How a Trump Mob Halted American Democracy," *Washington Post*, January 7, 2021, https://www.washingtonpost.com/graphics/2021/politics/trump-insurrection-capitol/.

4 McMaster, "Preserving Soldiers' Moral Character," 21–23.

5   Clark Mitchell, "Operational Culture Challenge: The Fallujah Peninsula, Iraq," in *Case Studies in Operational Culture*, ed. Paula Holmes-Eber and Marcus J. Mainz (Quantico, VA: Marine Corps University Press, 2014), 11–12.

6   Ibid., 13.

7   Charles Miller, "ADF Views on Islam: Does Cultural Sensitivity Training Matter?," *Australian Army Journal* XIII, no. 1 (2016), 36–43.

8   Prescott et al., *Ordinary Soldiers*, 9, 12–15.

9   GC IV, art. 35.

10   Shane Darcy, "The Evolution of Belligerent Reprisals," *Military Law Review* 175 (2003): 195.

11   *In the Criminal Proceedings against the Teacher N and the Criminal Justice Secretary Z,* Judgment of the State Court in Darmstadt of March 10, 1956 (No. 429), trans. Andre Becker, translation reproduced in Prescott et al., *Ordinary Soldiers*, 30–38.

12   Ibid., 15.

13   Ibid., 52n53.

14   Jenks, "The Efficacy of the U.S. Army's Law of War Training Program."

15   Andrew M. Bell, "Military Culture and Restraint toward Civilians in War: Examining the Ugandan Civil Wars," *Security Studies* 25, no. 3 (2016): 503–9.

16   Ibid., 507.

17   Sebastian Junger, *War* (New York: Twelve, 2010), 160.

18   Ibid., 161–62.

19   S. Alexander Halsam, Anne O'Brien, Jolanda Jetten, Karine Vormedal, and Sally Penna, "Taking the Strain: Social Identity, Social Support, and the Experience of Stress," *British Journal of Social Psychology* 44 (2005): 362–65.

20   Greg Jaffe, "The Cursed Platoon," *Washington Post*, July 2, 2020, https://www.washingtonpost.com/podcasts/post-reports/the-cursed-platoon-part-1/.

21   Ibid.

22   Elisabeth Jean Wood, "Armed Groups and Sexual Violence: When Is Wartime Rape Rare?," *Politics & Society* 37, no. 1 (March 2009): 140–42, 145–52.

23   Sandy Milne, "Defence to Streamline Learning through VR, Gaming Technologies," DefenceConnect, May 27, 2020, https://www.defenceconnect.com.au/key-enablers/6164-defence-to-streamline-learning-through-vr-gaming-technologies.

24   Jody M. Prescott, "Building the Ethical Cyber Commander and the Law of Armed Conflict," *Rutgers Computer & Technology Law Journal* 40 (2014): 42–77.

25   "Technical Exercises" and "News & Events," CybExer Technologies, https://cybexer.com (accessed November 27, 2020).

26   Laurie Almann, Zoom interview with author, November 27, 2020.

27   See "CybExer Conducted Strategic Table-Top Exercise for Prague Security Studies Institute Cyber Security Academy," CybExer Technologies, October 9, 2020, https://cybexer.com/cybexer-conducted-strategic-table-top-exercise-for-prague-security-studies-institute-cyber-security-academy/.

28   Almann interview.

29   49 United States Code Annotated § 1154(b) (2018); 49 Code of Federal Regulations § 835.2 (2020).

30   Prescott, "Tactical Implementation of Rules of Engagement," 250–53.

31   NATO, *ATrainP-2, Training in the Law of Armed Conflict*, ver. 1 (Brussels: NATO Standardization Office, June 2019), 1-3, B-1, C-1, D-1–D-2, F-1–F-124.

REFERENCES

49 Code of Federal Regulations § 835.2 (2020).

49 United States Code Annotated § 1154(b) (2018).

Adjutant-General's Office, US War Department. *General Orders No. 100, Instructions for the Government of Armies of the United States in the Field*. New York: D. van Nostrand, 1863. https://archive.org/details/governarmies00unitrich/page/10/mode/2up.

Anathan, S., and S. Inderjit. "Evaluating the Command Climate in Military Units." *European Journal of Educational Sciences* 1, no. 3 (September 2014): 165–73.

Aragon, David K. "The Challenge of Surviving within the Special Operations Culture." In *Case Studies of Operational Culture*, edited by Paula Holmes-Eber and Marcus J. Mainz, 7–10. Quantico, VA: Marine Corps University Press, 2014.

Baker, Peter. "For Obama, Syria Chemical Attack Shows Risk of 'Deals with Dictators.'" *New York Times*. April 9, 2017. https://www.nytimes.com/2017/04/09/us/politics/obama-syria-chemical-weapons.html.

Barnes, Christopher M., John Schaubroeck, Megan Huth, and Sonia Ghumman. "Lack of Sleep and Unethical Conduct." *Organizational Behavior and Human Decision Processes* 115 (2011): 169–80.

Bastian, Brock, Jolanda Jetten, and Helena R. M. Radke. "Cyber-Dehumanization: Violent Video Game Play Diminishes Our Humanity." *Journal of Experimental Social Psychology* 48 (2012): 486–91.

Batchelor, James. "Can Video Games Depict War Responsibly?" *Gamesindustry.biz*. May 7, 2020. https://www.gamesindustry.biz/articles/2020-05-07-war-and-video-games.

Bates, Elizabeth Stubbins. "Towards Effective Military Training in International Humanitarian Law." *International Review of the Red Cross* 96, nos. 895/896 (2014): 795–816.

BBC News. "US Soldier Admits Murdering Girl." February 22, 2007. http://news.bbc.co.uk/2/hi/americas/6384781.stm.

———. "Royal Navy's First Crewless Boat Ready for Testing." June 24, 2020. https://www.bbc.com/news/uk-53161264.

Bell, Andrew M. "Military Culture and Restraint toward Civilians in War: Examining the Ugandan Civil Wars." *Security Studies* 25, no. 3 (2016): 488–518.

Bell, Andrew M., and Fionna Terry. "Combatant Rank and Socialization to Norms of Restraint: Examining the Australian and Philippine Armies." *International Interactions* 59, no. 4 (2021): 1–29.

Blank, Laurie R. "Examining the Role of Law of War Training in International Criminal Accountability." *Utah Law Review* 2017, no. 4, article 6 (2017): 747–69.

Blank, Laurie R., and Gregory P. Noone. *Law of War Training, Resources for Military and Civilian Leaders*, 2nd ed. Washington, DC: United States Institute of Peace Press, 2013.

Blok, Stef. "The International Criminal Court Must Do Better. Reforms Are Urgently Needed." *Washington Post*. December 2, 2019. https://www.washingtonpost.com/opinions/2019/12/02/international-criminal-court-must-do-better-reforms-are-urgently-needed/.

Boal, Mark. "The Kill Team: How U.S. Soldiers in Afghanistan Murdered Innocent Civilians." *Rolling Stone*. March 28, 2011. https://www.rollingstone.com/politics/politics-news/the-kill-team-how-u-s-soldiers-in-afghanistan-murdered-innocent-civilians-169793/.

Boddens Hosang, J. F. R. *Rules of Engagement and the International Law of Military Operations*. New York: Oxford University Press, 2020.

Bralley, Neal H. "ILE: A New System for CGSC Students." *Army Logistician* 38, no. 1 (January/February 2006). https://alu.army.mil/alog/issues/JanFeb06/ile_cgsc.html.

Brassil, Denielle. "Increasing Compliance with International Humanitarian Law through Dissemination." *University of Western Australia Law Review* 39, no. 1 (2015): 83–109.

Brockmeier, Sarah, Oliver Stuenkel, and Marcos Tourinho. "The Impact of the Libya Intervention Debates on Norms of Protection." *Global Society* 30, no. 1 (2015): 113–33.

Brown, Gary, Daniel Greenberg, Seth Hudson, and Kurt Sanger. "Rules of the (Video) Game: IHL on the Virtual Battlefield." *American Society of International Law Proceedings* 109 (2015): 55–60.

Burkhart, Todd, and Rob Williamson. "Incorporating Law of Armed Conflict Training into Afghanistan's Special Forces' Curriculum." *Army Press Online Journal* 1615 (2016): 1–7. https://www.armyupress.army.mil/Journals/Military-Review/Online-Exclusive/2016-Online-Exclusive-Articles/Incorporating-Law-of-Armed-Conflict-Training/.

Castano, Emanuele, Bernhard Leidner, and Patrycja Slawata. "Social Identification Processes, Group Dynamics and the Behaviour of Combatants." *International Review of the Red Cross* 90, no. 870 (June 2008): 259–71.

CBS News. "Whiskey and Golf before Rape-Murder?" August 7, 2006. https://www.cbsnews.com/news/whiskey-and-golf-before-rape-murder/.

CybExer Technologies. "Technical Exercises" and "News and Events." https://cybexer.com (accessed November 27, 2020).

———. "CybExer Conducted Strategic Table-Top Exercise for Prague Security Studies Institute Cyber Security Academy." October 9, 2020. https://cybexer.com/cybexer-conducted-strategic-table-top-exercise-for-prague-security-studies-institute-cyber-security-academy/.

Dalgaard-Nielsen, Anja, and Kirstine Falster Holm. "Supersoldiers or Rulebreakers? Unpacking the Mind-Set of Special Operations Forces." *Armed Forces & Society* 45, no. 4 (2019): 591–611.

Daley, Paul. "Brereton War Crimes Report Fallout: What Now for Australia's Elite Special Forces?" *The Guardian*. November 19, 2020. https://www.theguardian.com/australia-news/2020/nov/19/brereton-war-crimes-report-fallout-what-now-for-australias-elite-special-forces.

Darcy, Shane. "The Evolution of Belligerent Reprisals." *Military Law Review* 175 (2003): 184–251.

DeCzege, Huba Wass. "The School of Advanced Military Studies: An Accident of History." *Military Review* 89, no. 4 (July/August 2009): 102–7.

Dehn, John C. "Institutional Advocacy, Constitutional Obligations, and Professional Responsibilities: Arguments for Government Lawyering without Glasses." *Columbia Law Review Sidebar* 110 (2010): 73–88.

De White, Melissa. "In a War Perceived as Just, Many Americans Excuse Soldiers Who Commit War Crimes, Stanford Scholar Finds." *Stanford News.* December 9, 2019. https://news.stanford.edu/2019/12/09/war-perceived-just-many-americans-excuse-war-criminals/.

Dickinson, Laura A. "Military Lawyers on the Battlefield: An Empirical Account of International Law Compliance." *American Journal of International Law* 104, no. 1 (2010): 1–28.

DiMeglio, Richard P. "Training Army Judge Advocates to Advise Commanders as Operational Law Attorneys." *Boston College Law Review* 54, no. 3 (2013): 1185–206.

Doty, Joseph, and Joe Gelineau. "Command Climate." *Army Magazine* 58, no. 7 (July 2008): 22–24. https://www.ausa.org/sites/default/files/FC_Doty_0708.pdf.

Falk, Richard Falk. "Opening the Other Eye: Charles Taylor and Selective Accountability." *Al Jazeera.* May 1, 2012. https://www.aljazeera.com/opinions/2012/5/1/opening-the-other-eye-charles-taylor-and-selective-accountability/.

Farnsworth, Clyde H. "Canada Ends Top Regiment after Charges." *New York Times.* January 25, 1995.

Fitzgerald, David. "Vietnam, Iraq and the Rebirth of Counter-Insurgency." *Irish Studies in International Affairs* 21 (2010): 149–59.

Frederick, Bryan, and David E. Johnson. *The Continued Evolution of U.S. Law of Armed Conflict Implementation.* Santa Monica, CA: RAND Corporation, 2015.

Gallup. "In Depth: Topics A to Z, Religion." https://news.gallup.com/poll/1690/religion.aspx (accessed July 26, 2020).

Garamone, Jim. "Noncommissioned Officers Give Big Advantage to U.S. Military." *Defense.* November 7, 2019. https://www.defense.gov/Explore/News/Article/Article/2011393/noncommissioned-officers-give-big-advantage-to-us-military/#:~:text=%22NCOs%20are%20the%20doers%2C%22,of%20those%20in%20their%20charge.%22.

Geneva Convention for the Amelioration of the Condition of Wounded, Sick and Shipwrecked Members of the Armed Forces at Sea. Adopted August 12, 1949, entered into force October 21, 1950. 75 UNTS 31 (GC I).

Geneva Convention for the Amelioration of the Condition of Wounded, Sick and Shipwrecked Members of the Armed Forces in the Field. Adopted August 12, 1949, entered into force October 21, 1950. 75 UNTS 85 (GC II).

Geneva Convention Relevant to the Treatment of Prisoners of War. Adopted August 12, 1949, entered into force October 21, 1950. 75 UNTS 135 (GC III).

Geneva Convention Relevant to the Protection of Civilian Persons in Time of War. Adopted August 12, 1949, entered into force October 21, 1950. 75 UNTS 287 (GC IV).

Golden, Tim. "Years after 2 Afghans Died, Abuse Case Falters." *New York Times.* February 13, 2006. https://www.nytimes.com/2006/02/13/us/years-after-2-afghans-died-abuse-case-falters.html.

Greenberg Research, Inc. *The People on War Report, ICRC Worldwide Consultation on the Rules of War.* October 1999. https://www.icrc.org/en/doc/assets/files/other/globalreport.pdf.

Halsam, Alexander, Anne O'Brien, Jolanda Jetten, Karine Vormedal, and Sally Penna. "Taking the Strain: Social Identity, Social Support, and the Experience of Stress." *British Journal of Social Psychology* 44 (2005): 355–70.

Hansen, Victor M. "Developing Empirical Methodologies to Study Law of War Violations." *Willamette Journal of International Law and Dispute Resolution* 16, no. 2 (2008): 342–85.

Hansler, Jennifer. "Pompeo Slams International Criminal Court Decision to Authorize Afghanistan War Crimes Investigation." *CNN.* March 5, 2020. https://www.cnn.com/2020/03/05/politics/icc-afghanistan-pompeo/index.html.

Hassan, Falih, and Jane Arraf. "Blackwater's Bullets Scarred Iraqis. Trump's Pardon Renewed the Pain." *New York Times.* December 23, 2020. https://www.nytimes.com/2020/12/23/world/middleeast/blackwater-trump-pardon.html.

Headquarters, Department of the Army (HQDA). *Field Manual 27-10, The Law of Land Warfare.* Washington, DC: HQDA, 1956.

———. *Army Regulation 600-20, Army Command Policy.* Washington, DC: HQDA, 2006.

———. *Army Regulation 350-1, Army Training and Leader Development.* Washington, DC: HQDA, 2007.

———. *Army Regulation 350-1, Army Training and Leader Development.* Washington, DC: HQDA, 2017.

———. *Army Doctrine Publication 6-22 C1, Army Leadership and the Profession.* Washington, DC: HQDA, 2019.

HQDA and Headquarters, United States Marine Corps (HUSMC). *Field Manual 27-10/Marine Corps Tactical Publication 11-10C, The Commander's Handbook on the Law of Land Warfare.* Washington, DC: HQDA and HUSMC, 2019.

Henckaerts, Jean-Marie, and Louise Doswald-Beck, *Customary International Law, Volume I: Rules.* Cambridge: Cambridge University Press, 2005.

Holowka, Darren W., Erika J. Wolf, Brian P. Marx, Kristen M. Foley, Danny G. Kaloupek, and Terrence M. Keane. "Associations among Personality, Combat Exposure and Wartime Atrocities." *Psychology of Violence* 2, no. 3 (2012): 260–72.

Human Rights Watch. "Human Rights Watch Briefing Note for the Eighteenth Session of the International Criminal Court Assembly of States Parties." November 2019. https://www.hrw.org/sites/default/files/news_attachments/asp_final_en_0.pdf.

ICRC. "Law of Armed Conflict, Basic Knowledge, Lesson 1." 2002. https://www.icrc.org/en/doc/assets/files/other/law1_final.pdf.

———. *Integrating the Law, Publication Ref. 0900.* Geneva: ICRC, May 2007. https://www.icrc.org/en/doc/assets/files/other/icrc-002-0900.pdf.

———. "Video Games and Law of War." September 27, 2013. https://www.icrc.org/en/document/video-games-get-real.

———. "Video Games That Protect Civilians." October 16, 2017. https://www.youtube.com/watch?v=0nSpXOAiYr8&feature=youtu.be.

———. Statutes of the International Committee of the Red Cross. Adopted December 21, 2017, entered into force January 1, 2018. https://www.icrc.org/en/document/statutes-international-committee-red-cross-0.

———. "Let's Get Real." April 29, 2019. https://blogs.icrc.org/inspired/2019/04/29/half-bohemia-interactive-s-net-revenue-laws-war-dlc-2017-donated-icrc/.

———. *Millennials On War, Publication Ref. 4444.* Geneva: ICRC, January 2020. https://shop.icrc.org/millennials-on-war-pdf-en.

———. "IHL Database, Rule 140. Principle of Reciprocity." https://ihl-databases.icrc.org/customary-ihl/eng/docs/v1_rul_rule140.

———. "Fundamentals of IHL." https://casebook.icrc.org/law/fundamentals-ihl# (accessed November 24, 2020).

Independent Institute for Administration and Civil Society Studies. "Public Opinion in Iraq, First Poll Following Abu Ghraib Revelations." June 15, 2004. https://www.globalpolicy.org/invasion-and-war/iraqi-public-opinion-and-polls.html.

Inspector-General of the Australian Defence Force (I-GADF). *Afghanistan Inquiry Report.* Canberra: I-GADF, 2020 (The Brereton Report).

International Commission on Intervention and State Sovereignty. *The Responsibility to Protect—Report of the International Commission on Intervention and State Sovereignty.* Ottawa: International Development Research Centre, 2001.

Jackson, Kimberly, Katherine L. Kidder, Sean Mann, William H. Waggy II, Natasha Lander, and S. Rebecca Zimmerman. *Raising the Flag—Implications of U.S. Military Approaches to General and Flag Officer Development.* Santa Monica, CA: RAND Corporation, 2020.

Jaffe, Greg. "The Cursed Platoon." *Washington Post.* July 2, 2020. https://www.washingtonpost.com/graphics/2020/national/clint-lorance-platoon-afghanistan/.

Jenks, Chris. "The Efficacy of the U.S. Army's Law of War Training Program." *Articles of War,* Lieber Institute at West Point (blog). October 14, 2020. https://lieber.westpoint.edu/efficacy-u-s-armys-law-of-war-training-program/.

Jones, David E., Franca Jones, Laura Suttinger, Ayessa Toler, Patricia Hammond, and Steven Medina. "Placement of Combat Stress Teams in Afghanistan: Reducing Barriers to Care." *Military Medicine* 178, no. 2 (2013): 121–25.

The Judge Advocate General's Legal Center and School (TJAGLCS). *Commander's Legal Handbook, Misc. Pub. 27-8.* Charlottesville, VA: TJAGSLC, 2019.

Junger, Sebastian. *War.* New York: Twelve, 2010.

Kelloway, E. Kevin, Nick Turner, Julian Barling, and Catherine Loughlin. "Transformational Leadership and Employee Psychological Well-being: The Mediating Role of Employee Trust in Leadership." *Work & Stress* 26, no. 1 (January/March 2012): 39–55.

Keneally, Meghan. "Why the US Got Involved in Afghanistan—and Why It's Been Difficult to Get Out." *ABC News.* August 21, 2017. https://abcnews.go.com/US/us-involved-afghanistan-difficult/story?id=49341264.

Ketz, Brian, and Jody Prescott. "Ordinary Soldiers." *Legacy of Learning Series,* Norwich University. April 29, 2020. https://attendee.gotowebinar.com/recording/67643461427341839 (webinar ID 576-589-243).

Knaus, Christopher. "Australian Special Forces Involved in Murder of 39 Afghan Civilians, War Crimes Report Alleges." *The Guardian.* November 19, 2020. https://www.theguardian.com/australia-news/2020/nov/19/australian-special-forces-involved-in-of-39-afghan-civilians-war-crimes-report-alleges.

Knowles, Emily, and Jahara Matisek. "Is Human Rights Training Working with Foreign Militaries? No One Knows and That's O.K." *War on the Rocks.* May 12, 2020. https://warontherocks.com/2020/05/is-human-rights-training-working-with-foreign-militaries-no-one-knows-and-thats-o-k/.

Kowalski, Evan, and Jody M. Prescott. "Hybrid Conflict and Effective Leadership Training." *Journal of Military Learning* 3, no. 2. (October 2019): 74–95. https://www.armyupress.army.mil/Journals/Journal-of-Military-Learning/Journal-of-Military-Learning-Archives/October-2019/Kowalski-hybrid-conflict/.

Lacina, Bethany, and Nils Peter Gleditsch. "Monitoring Trends in Global Combat: A New Dataset of Battle Deaths." *European Journal of Population* 21 (2005): 145–66.

Library of Congress. "Brief Descriptions and Expanded Essays of National Film Registry Titles." https://www.loc.gov/programs/national-film-preservation-board/film-registry/descriptions-and-essays/ (accessed September 6, 2020).

Lopez, C. Todd. "Study Focuses on Mental Health of Force in Afghanistan." *U.S. Army.* May 20, 2011. https://www.army.mil/article/56845/study_focuses_on_mental_health_of_force_in_afghanistan.

Luscombe, Richard. "Navy Seal Pardoned of War Crimes by Trump Described by Colleagues as 'Freaking Evil.'" *The Guardian*. December 27, 2019. https://www.theguardian.com/us-news/2019/dec/27/eddie-gallagher-trump-navy-seal-iraq.

MacManus, Deidre, Kimberlie Dean, Margaret Jones, Roberto J. Rona, Neil Greenberg, Lisa Hull, Tom Fahy, Simon Wessely, and Nicola T. Fear. "Violent Offending by UK Military Personnel Deployed to Iraq and Afghanistan: A Data Linkage Cohort Study." *Lancet* 381 (2013): 907–17.

Magruder, Daniel L. *Counterinsurgency, Security Forces, and the Identification Problem: Distinguishing Friend from Foe.* London: Routledge, 2018.

Margalit, Alon. *Investigating Civilian Casualties in Times of Armed Conflict and Belligerent Occupation: Manoeuvring between Legal Regimes and Paradigms for the Use of Force.* Leiden: Brill Nijhoff, 2018.

Mastroanni, George R. "The Person-Situation Debate: Implications for Military Leadership and Civil-Military Relations." *Journal of Military Ethics* 10, no. 1 (2011): 2–16.

McCammon, Sarah. "The Warfare May Be Remote but the Trauma Is Real." *NPR*. April 24, 2017. https://www.npr.org/2017/04/24/525413427/for-drone-pilots-warfare-may-be-remote-but-the-trauma-is-real.

McMaster, H. R. "Preserving Soldiers' Moral Character in Counter-insurgency Operations." In *Ethics Education for Irregular Warfare*, edited by Don Carrick, James Connelly, and Paul Robinson, 15–54. Farnham: Ashgate, 2009.

Miller, Alex. "How Video Games Are Saving Those Who Served." *Wired*. October 20, 2020. https://www.wired.com/story/video-games-therapy-veterans-ptsd-treatment/.

Miller, Charles. "ADF Views on Islam: Does Cultural Sensitivity Training Matter?" *Australian Army Journal* XIII, no. 1 (2016): 35–50.

Milne, Sandy. "Defence to Streamline Learning through VR, Gaming Technologies." *DefenceConnect*. May 27, 2020. https://www.defenceconnect.com.au/key-enablers/6164-defence-to-streamline-learning-through-vr-gaming-technologies.

Minai, Keisuke. "Encouragement of Learning through War Video Games as an Intelligible Textbook on International Humanitarian Law." *Cornell International Law Journal* 52 (2020): 644–73.

Mitchell, Clark. "Operational Culture Challenge: The Fallujah Peninsula, Iraq." In *Case Studies in Operational Culture*, edited by Paula Holmes-Eber and Marcus J. Mainz, 11–14. Quantico, VA: Marine Corps University Press, 2014.

Moffett, Luke, Dug Cubie, and Andrew Godden. "Bringing the Battlefield into the Classroom: Using Video Games to Teach and Assess International Humanitarian Law." *Law Teacher* 51, no. 4 (2017): 499–514.

Mulrine, Anna. "Pentagon Had Red Flags about Command Climate in 'Kill Team' Stryker Brigade." *Christian Science Monitor*. October 28, 2010. https://www.csmonitor.com/USA/Military/2010/1028/Pentagon-had-red-flags-about-command-climate-in-kill-team-Stryker-brigade.

Muñoz-Rojas, Daniel, and Jean-Jacques Frésard. "The Roots of Behaviour in War: Understanding and Preventing IHL Violations." *International Review of the Red Cross* 853 (March 2004): 189–206.

Murphy, John F. "Will-o'-the-Wisp? The Search for Law in Non-International Armed Conflicts." *International Legal Studies* 88 (2012): 15–39.

NATO. *ATrainP-2, Training in the Law of Armed Conflict*, Ver. 1. Brussels: NATO Standardization Office, June 2019.

Nordmo, Morten, Olav Kjellevold Olsen, Jørn Hetland, Roar Espevik, Arnold Bastiaan Bakker, and Ståle Pallesen. "Daily Sleep Quality and Naval Work Performance: The Role of Leadership." *International Maritime Health* 70, no. 4 (2019): 202–9.

Nyberg, A., L. Alfredsson, T. Theorell, H. Westerlund, J. Vahtera, and M. Kivimäki. "Managerial Leadership and Ischaemic Heart Disease among Employees: The Swedish WOLF Study." *Occupational and Environmental Medicine* 66, no. 1 (January 2009): 51–55.

Office of the Command Surgeon, [redacted], and Office of the Surgeon General, US Army Medical Command. *Mental Health Advisory Team (MHAT) V, Operation Enduring Freedom 8, Afghanistan.* February 14, 2008. https://armymedicine.health.mil/Reports.

Office of the General Counsel (OGC), Department of Defense. *Department of Defense Law of War Manual.* Washington, DC: OGC, December 2016. https://dod.defense. gov/Portals/1/Documents/pubs/DoD%20Law%20of%20War%20Manual%20-%20June%202015%20Updated%20Dec%202016.pdf?ver=2016-12-13-172036-190.

———. Department of Defense Directive 2311.01. "DoD Law of War Program." July 2, 2020. https://www.esd.whs.mil/Portals/54/Documents/DD/issuances/dodd/231101p.pdf?ver=2020-07-02-143157-007.

Office of the Surgeon General, US Army Medical Command; Office of the Command Surgeon, HQ, USCENTCOM; and Office of the Command Surgeon, US Forces Afghanistan (USFOR-A). *Joint Mental Health Advisory Team 7 (J-MHAT 7), Operation Enduring Freedom 2020, Afghanistan.* February 22, 2011. https://armymedicine.health. mil/Reports.

———. *Mental Health Advisory Team 9 (MHAT 9) Operation Enduring Freedom 2013, Afghanistan.* October 10, 2013. https://armymedicine.health.mil/Reports.

Office of the Surgeon, Multi-National Force-Iraq, and Office of the Surgeon General, US Army Medical Command. *Mental Health Advisory Team (MHAT) IV, Operation Iraqi Freedom 05-07, Final Report.* November 17, 2006. http://www.peaceispatriotic.org/articles/MHAT_IV_Report_17NOV06.pdf.

———. *Mental Health Advisory Team (MHAT) IV, Operation Iraqi Freedom 05-07, Final Report.* November 17, 2006. https://ntrl.ntis.gov/NTRL/dashboard/searchResults/titleDetail/PB2010103335.xhtml.

———. *Mental Health Advisory Team (MHAT) V, Operation Iraqi Freedom 06-08.* February 14, 2008. https://apps.dtic.mil/dtic/tr/fulltext/u2/a519676.pdf.

Olsen, Olav Kjellevold, Ståle Pallessen, and Jarle Eid. "The Impact of Partial Sleep Deprivation on Moral Reasoning in Military Officers." *Sleep* 33, no. 8 (2010): 1086–90.

Oppman, Patrick. "Soldier Found Guilty of Murdering Afghans, Sentenced to Life." *CNN.* November 11, 2011. https://www.cnn.com/2011/11/10/justice/soldier-murder-rial/index.html.

Paterson, Patrick. *Training Surrogate Forces in International Humanitarian Law: Lessons from Peru, Colombia, El Salvador, and Iraq, JSOU Report 16-9.* Tampa, FL: Joint Special Operations University Press, 2016.

PBS. "Meet the Participants, My Lai." https://www.pbs.org/wgbh/americanexperience/features/my-lai-selected-men-involved-my-lai/ (accessed November 24, 2020).

Peristerakis, Julia. "Jody Williams and the Campaign to Ban Landmines." Canadian Museum for Human Rights. https://humanrights.ca/story/jody-williams-and-the-campaign-to-ban-landmines#:~:text=On%20October%2010%2C%201997%2C%20less,Ban%20Landmines%20and%20Jody%20Williams (accessed October 1, 2020).

Petrigh, Cynthia. *Even Wars Have Limits: An IHL Training Manual, Based on the Training Designed and Delivered for the European Union Training Mission in Mali (EUTM), Koulikouro Training Camp.* Paris: Beyond Peace, 2014.

Prescott, Jody, Waitman Wade Beorn, Jennifer Ciardelli, David Frey, and Gretchen Skidmore. *Ordinary Soldiers: A Study in Ethics, Law, and Leadership.* Washington, DC: United States Holocaust Memorial Museum and Center for Holocaust and Genocide Studies at West Point, 2014. https://www.ushmm.org/m/pdfs/20140830-ordinary-soldiers-case-study.pdf.

Prescott, Jody M. "Building the Ethical Cyber Commander and the Law of Armed Conflict." *Rutgers Computer & Technology Journal,* 40 (2014): 42–77.

———. "Litigating Genocide: A Consideration of the International Criminal Court in Light of the German Jews' Legal Response to Nazi Persecution, 1933–1941." *Maine Law Review* 51 (1999): 297–339.

———. "The North Atlantic Treaty Organization." In *An Institutional Approach to the Responsibility to Protect,* edited by Gentian Zyberi, 338–61. London: Cambridge University Press, 2014.

———. "Tactical Implementation of Rules of Engagement in a Multinational Force Reality." In *U.S. Military Operations: Law, Policy, and Practice,* edited by Geoffrey S. Corn, Rachel E. VanLandingham, and Shane R. Reeves, 249–74. New York: Oxford University Press, 2016.

———. "Training in the Law of Armed Conflict—a NATO Perspective." *Journal of Military Ethics* 7, no. 1 (March 2008): 66–75.

Prescott, Jody M., and Jerry Dunlap. "Law of War and Rules of Engagement Training for the Objective Force: A Proposed Methodology for Training Role-Players." *Army Lawyer* (July 2000): 43–47.

Protocol Additional to the Geneva Conventions of 12 August 1949, and Relating to the Protection of Victims of International Armed Conflicts. Adopted June 8, 1977, entered into force December 7, 1978. 1125 UNTS 3 (AP I).

Rayburn, Joel D., and Frank K. Sobchak (eds.). *The U.S. Army in the Iraq War, Volume 1: Invasion–Insurgency–Civil War.* Carlisle Barracks, PA: United States Army War College Press, 2019.Reuters. "EA Profit, Revenue Top Estimates on Strong 'Battlefield 1' Sales." January 31, 2017. https://www.reuters.com/article/us-electronic-arts-results/ea-profit-revenue-top-estimates-on-strong-battlefield-1-sales-idUSKBN15F2LQ.

Richard, Theodore T. *Unofficial United States Guide to the First Additional Protocol to the Geneva Conventions of 12 August 1949.* Maxwell Air Force Base, AL: Air University Press, 2019.

Roberts, Adam. "The Law of War: Problems of Implementation in Contemporary Conflicts." *Duke Journal of Comparative & International Law* 6 (1995): 11–78.

Roberts, David Lloyd. "Teaching the Law of Armed Conflict to Armed Forces: Personal Reflections." *International Law Studies* 82 (2006): 121–34.

Robles, C. J. "New Survey Finds 75% of Gamers Play Video Games to Maintain Mental Health." *Tech Times.* October 22, 2020. https://www.techtimes.com/articles/253551/20201022/new-survey-finds-75-gamers-play-video-games-maintain-mental.htm.

Rome Statute of the International Criminal Court. Adopted July 17, 1998, entered into force July 1, 2002. 2187 UNTS 90, no. 38544.

Roper Center for Public Opinion Research. "American Soldiers Studies of WWII." https://ropercenter.cornell.edu/american-soldiers-studies-wwii (accessed August 21, 2020).

Rosen, Richard D. "The Judge Advocate General's School, U.S. Army: 50 Years in Charlottesville." *Virginia Lawyer* (December 2001): 14–18. https://www.vsb.org/docs/valawyermagazine/dec01rosen.pdf.

Rossi, Altea. "Training Armed Forces in IHL: Just a Matter of Law?" *OpinioJuris* (blog). October 8, 2020. http://opiniojuris.org/2020/10/08/training-armed-forces-in-ihl-just-a-matter-of-law/.

Sandoz, Yves. "The International Committee of the Red Cross as Guardian of International Humanitarian Law." *ICRC*. December 31, 1998. https://www.icrc.org/en/doc/resources/documents/misc/about-the-icrc-311298.htm#:~:text=Article%205%20of%20the%20Statutes,alleged%20breaches%20of%20that%20law%E2%80%9D%20.

Savage, Charlie, and Elisabeth Bumiller. "An Iraqi Massacre, a Light Sentence, and a Question of Military Justice." *New York Times*. January 27, 2012. https://www.nytimes.com/2012/01/28/us/an-iraqi-massacre-a-light-sentence-and-a-question-of-military-justice.html.

Schlosser, Nicholas J. *The Surge: 2007–2008*. Washington, DC: US Army Center of Military History, 2017.

Schmitt, Michael N. "Investigating Violations of International Law in Armed Conflict." *Harvard National Security Journal* 2 (2011): 31–84.

Schumacher, Julie A., and Kenneth E. Leonard. "Husbands' and Wives' Marital Adjustment, Verbal Aggression, and Physical Aggression as Longitudinal Predictors of Physical Aggression in Early Marriage." *Journal of Consulting and Clinical Psychology* 73, no. 1 (2005): 28–37.

Seiler, Stefan, Andreas Fischer, and Sibylle A. Voegtli. "Developing Moral Decision-Making Competence: A Quasi-Experimental Intervention Study in the Swiss Armed Forces." *Ethics and Behavior* 21, no. 6 (2011): 452–70.

Sharbutt, Jay. "'Platoon' Is Top Film; Newman Is Best Actor." *Los Angeles Times*. March 31, 1987. https://www.latimes.com/archives/la-xpm-1987-03-31-mn-1504-story.html.

Shirer, William L. *The Rise and Fall of the Third Reich: A History of Nazi Germany*. New York: Simon and Schuster, 1960.

Slavin, Erik. "Navy Medicine CO Fired for Poor Command Climate." *Stars and Stripes*. April 12, 2012. https://www.stripes.com/navy-medicine-co-fired-for-poor-command-climate-1.174217#:~:text=YOKOSUKA%20NAVAL%20BASE%2C%20Japan%20%E2%80%94%20The,April%206%20by%20Rear%20Adm.

Smith, Rupert. *The Utility of Force: The Art of War in the Modern World*. New York: Knopf, 2007.

Stephens, Dale. "Behaviour in War: The Place of Law, Moral Inquiry and Self-Identity." *International Review of the Red Cross* 96, nos. 895/896 (2014): 751–73.

Stouffer, Samuel A. "Men from the 101st Airborne, European Theater of Operations." *Research Branch, Information and Education Division, War Department*. May 1944. https://ropercenter.cornell.edu/ipoll/study/31089936.

Stratton, Anita. "Roleplayers and Technology Enhance Soldier Training." *Defense Visual Information Distribution Service*. August 24, 2015. https://www.dvidshub.net/news/174262/roleplayers-and-technology-enhance-soldier-training.

Sullivan, Charles S. "Game-Changing Strategies for Counterinsurgency and Complex Joint Operations." In *Airpower in Afghanistan 2005–10: The Air Commanders' Perspectives*, edited by Dag Hendriksen, 157–234. Maxwell Air Force Base, AL: Air University Press, 2014.

SWI swissinfo.ch. "Red Cross Develops War Video Games—with Rules." March 19, 2019. https://www.youtube.com/watch?v=wQc4-vFJ2Oc.

Taguba, Antonio M. *AR 15-6 Investigation of the 800th Military Police Brigade*. Baghdad: Coalition Forces Land Component Command, 2004. https://www.thetorturedatabase.org/document/ar-15-6-investigation-800th-military-police-investigating-officer-mg-antonio-taguba-taguba-.

Talbert, Matthew, and Jessica Wolfendale. *War Crimes: Causes, Excuses, and Blame*. New York: Oxford University Press, 2019.

Terry, Fiona, and Brian McQuinn. *The Roots of Restraint in War*. Geneva: ICRC, 2018.

Thompson, Megan M., and Rakesh Jetly. "Battlefield Ethics Training: Integrating Ethical Scenarios in High-Intensity Military Field Exercises." *European Journal of Psychotraumatology* 5, no. 1 (2014): 1–10.

UN General Assembly Resolution 60/1. *2005 World Summit Outcome*. A/RES/60/1. September 16, 2005.

UN Security Council Resolution 1973. *On the Situation in the Libyan Arab Jamahiriya*. S/RES/1973. March 17, 2011.

US Army Command and General Staff College. "Law of War and Rules of Engagement Training Survey, No. 02-004." 2001.

US Army G-1, Personnel. "Army Command Climate Survey: Soldiers in TO&E Units, ver. 6.2." https://www.armyg1.army.mil/documents/CMD_Climate_Surveys/TOE-CCSv6.2%2006_2013.pdf (accessed August 23, 2020).

US Department of Defense. "Military Units, Army." https://www.defense.gov/Experience/Military-Units/Army/ (accessed August 17, 2020).

US General Accounting Office. "Military Readiness: Full Training Benefits from Army's Combat Training Centers Are Not Being Realized, GAO/NSIAD-99-210." September 1999. https://www.gao.gov/assets/230/228237.pdf.

Van Baarle, Eva, Laura Hartman, Desiree Verweij, Bert Molewijk, and Guy Widdershoven. "What Sticks? The Evaluation of a Train-the-Trainer Course in Military Ethics and Its Perceived Outcomes." *Journal of Military Ethics* 16, nos. 1/2 (2017): 56–77.

Vargas, Jose Antonio. "Virtual Reality Prepares Soldiers for Real War Young Warriors Say Video Shooter Games Helped Hone Their Skills." *Washington Post*. February 14, 2006. https://www.washingtonpost.com/archive/politics/2006/02/14/virtual-reality-prepares-soldiers-for-real-war-span-classbankheadyoung-warriors-say-video-shooter-games-helped-hone-their-skillsspan/15996806-3a4d-4374-b066-38c5f5c35659/.

Wallach, Evan J. "Pray Fire First Gentlemen of France: Has 21st Century Chivalry Been Subsumed by Humanitarian Law?" *Harvard National Security Journal* 3 (2012): 432–69.

Warner, Christopher H., and George Appenzeller. "Engaged Leadership—Linking the Professional Ethic and Battlefield Behaviors." *Military Review* 91 (September/October 2011): 61–69.

Warner, Christopher H., George N. Appenzeller, Angela Mobbs, Jessica R. Parker, Carolynn M. Warner, Thomas Grieger, and Charles W. Hoge. "Effectiveness of Battlefield-Ethics Training during Combat Deployment: A Programme Assessment." *Lancet* 378 (2011): 915–24.

Wilk, Joshua E., Paul D. Bliese, Jeffrey L. Thomas, Michael D. Wood, Dennis McGurk, Carl A. Castro, and Charles W. Hoge. "Unethical Battlefield Conduct Reported by Soldiers Serving in the Iraq War." *Journal of Nervous and Mental Disease* 201, no. 4 (2013): 259–65.

Willemin, Georges, and Roger Heacock. *The International Committee of the Red Cross, International Organization and the Evolution of World Society, Vol. 2*. The Hague: Martinus Nijhoff, 1984.

WIN/Gallup International Association. "People on War—2016 Survey." 2016. https://www.icrc.org/en/document/people-war-2016-background-and-methodology.

Wood, Elisabeth Jean. "Armed Groups and Sexual Violence: When Is Wartime Rape Rare?" *Politics & Society*, 37, no. 1 (March 2009): 131–62.

World Population Review. "World War Two Casualties by Country 2020." https://worldpopulationreview.com/country-rankings/world-war-two-casualties-by-country (accessed September 26, 2020).

Yardley, William. "Drug Use Cited in the Killings of 3 Civilians: Testimony in Afghan Case—Tapes Aired." *New York Times*. September 28, 2010.

———. "Soldier Is Given 24 Years in Civilian Afghan Deaths." *New York Times*. March 24, 2011.

INDEX